ZION

The First Pillar of Zion
The New and Everlasting Covenant

LARRY BARKDULL

Pillars of Zion Series Titles

Introduction: *Portrait of a Zion Person*

Book 1: *Zion—Our Origin and Our Destiny*

Book 2: *The First Pillar of Zion—The New and Everlasting Covenant*

Book 3: *The Second Pillar of Zion—The Oath and Covenant of the Priesthood*

Book 4: *The Third Pillar of Zion—The Law of Consecration*

Book 5: *The Pure in Heart*

Book 6: *No Poor among Them*

Pillars of Zion Publishing
Orem, Utah

Copyright and Permission

Copyright © 2009, 2013 Barkdull Marketing, Inc

Publishing Imprint: Pillars of Zion Publishing, a division of Barkdull Marketing, Inc. Licensed for publication and distributed by BestBooks Publishing and Distribution, Spanish Fork, Utah. Phone: 801.815.5349.

All Rights Reserved. No part of this book may be reproduced in any format or in any medium without the written permision from the publisher, BestBooks Publishing and Distribution.

Contact

Contact us at info@pillarsofzion.com
Visit our Website at www.PillarsOfZion.com

Disclaimer

This series is heavily documented with some 5,000 references and 400 works cited. Every effort has been made to achieve accuracy. This work is not an official publication of the Church of Jesus Christ of Latter-day Saints, and the views expressed within this work are the sole responsibility of the author and do not necessarily reflect the position of The Church of Jesus Christ of Latter-day Saints or any other entity.

LICENSE USE

1) If you received the free PDF version of the introduction to t he series *Portrait of a Zion Person,* you have the right to store it on your computer. You also have the right to share the PDF with as many people as you please, provided that neither they nor you use part or all of the content to disparage The Church of Jesus Christ of Latter-day Saints in any manner. Neither you nor anyone with whom you share the PDF has the right to change the content of the PDF.

2) If you purchased the printed book or a version of the book for an electronic reader, you do not have the right to share those versions of the book.

Refer all copyright and permissions issues to the contact above.

Library of Congress Cataloging Publication Data is on file at the Library of Congress.
ISBN: 978-1-937399-04-7

Dedication
To Elizabeth Barkdull
Ron and Bonnie McMillan
David and Lorelea Anderson
Paul and Sharon Meyers

Acknowledgments
My wife, Elizabeth, and I would like to acknowledge a number of people, who, in one way or another, lent their support for the creation of this project.

    Lawrence and Georgia Shaw
    Lance and Jozet Richardson
    Blaine and Kathy Yorgason
    Scot and Maurine Proctor
    Clay Gorton
    Ted Gibbons
    Grover Cardon
    Gary and Bonnie Leavitt
    Bud and Barbara Poduska
    Dee Jay Bawden
    Steve Glenn
    Gavon and Tanya Barkdull

Production Staff
Thanks to Eschler Editing for editorial and design work.

    Editors—Jay A. Parry and Michele Preisendorf
    Graphic Artist—Douglass Cole
    Typesetter—Sean Graham

Note about The Three Pillars of Zion
The complete Zion series contains seven books. The full bibliography, and index are included in each of the books for ease of referencing and navigation. Each volume includes its own table of contents except for the Introduction book, *Portrait of a Zion Person*, includes the table of contents for each volume in order to introduce the entire series.

Table of Contents

Book 2
The First Pillar of Zion—The New and Everlasting Covenant

Introduction 1

Section 1
Preface to the New and Everlasting Covenant 3

The Plan of Happiness	4
The Covenant of the Gods	4
Happiness Encompasses All That Is Good	5
Balancing Justice and Mercy	6
Placed beyond Our Enemies	6
How Mercy Appeases Justice	7
Experiencing Contrasts Leads to Happiness	7
Overview of the New and Everlasting Covenant	9
The Covenant of Justice	10
Who Are the Just, and How Are They Justified?	10
Justification and Agency	12
Celestial Law	13
Preserved, Perfected, and Sanctified by the Laws of God	15
Blessed As If We Understood	15
The Covenant of Mercy	16
Mercy and Grace	17
Justification	17
Purification	18
Sanctification	20
Our Responsibility	20
The Crucible—The Baptism of Fire	21
Purified and Sanctified to Make an Offering	22
Oneness or Unification	23
Oneness and the Law of Restoration	25
Restoration and Resurrection	25
Hundredfold Restoration	27
Oneness and Deliverance	27
Summary and Conclusion	28

Section 2
The New and Everlasting Covenant, The First Pillar of Zion 31
    The Structure of the Covenant   32
    The New and Everlasting Covenant As an Agreement   33
    1. Introduction   33
    2. The Covenant of Justice   34
    3. The Covenant of Mercy   35
    4. The Covenant of Baptism   36
        Agreement to Renew and Abide in the Covenant of Baptism   37
        Agreement to Live the Law of the Sabbath Day   38
    5. Agreement to Receive the Covenant of the Priesthood   40
        Worthy Men Agree to Be Ordained   40
        Ordained Men Agree to Magnify Their Calling   42
        Ordained Men Agree to Continued Faithfulness   43
    6. Abide in the Covenant to the End   44
        Blessings for Enduring to the End   44
        The Father's Guarantee   45
        Effective Signatures   45

Section 3
Abide in the Covenant 47
    The Leavening Power of the Doctrine of the Covenant   48
    The Covenant Separates Us from Babylon, or the World   49
    Zion People Are Distinguished by Observing the Sabbath Day   50
    Power in the Covenant   51
    Other Powers Manifested in the Covenant   53
    Safety in the Covenant   54
    Safety through Consecration in the Covenant   55
    The Great Discovery   57
    Examples of Safety in the Covenant   57
    Progressing in the Covenant   60
    Discovering the Relationship through Progression   61
    Order in the Covenant   62
    Order and Ordinances   63
    Order and Consecration   64
    Abide in the Covenant   64
    Abiding in the Covenant Summons Divine Love   66
    Abiding in the Covenant through the Sacrament   67
    Summary and Conclusion   67

Section 4
The New and Everlasting Covenant—The Holy Marriage 71
    Born to Marry   72
    The Parents' Responsibility and the Bride's Choice   73
    Requirements to Legalize the Covenant   74
    Initiating the Marriage Proposal   74
    Entering into the Covenant   75
    Bought with a Price   76
    The Marriage Contract   77
    The Gift of Value   79
    The Pledge   80
    The Cup to Seal the Covenant   81
    The Covenantal Feast   82
    The Father's Announcement   82
    The Bride's Veil   83
    The Friend of the Bridegroom   84
    Preparing for Each Other   85
    The Serious Nature of Preparing   87
    The Bride's Final Preparations   89
    Invitation to the Wedding   91
    The Wedding Processional   92
    Claiming the Bride   93
    The Wedding   94
    The Bridegroom's Plea   97
    Postlude   98

Bibliography 101
Index and Concordance 111
About the Author 137

Book 2
The First Pillar of Zion—The New and Everlasting Covenant

Introduction

In this second book of The Three Pillars of Zion series, we will examine in depth the first pillar of Zion: The New and Everlasting Covenant. We recall that the "law of the Church" (D&C 42) states that three covenants are sufficient to establish us as Zion people: "And ye shall hereafter receive church covenants, such as shall be sufficient to establish you, both here and in the New Jerusalem."[1] These covenants are:

1. The New and Everlasting Covenant. (D&C 132:4–7)
2. The Oath and Covenant of the Priesthood. (D&C 84:33–44)
3. The Law of Consecration. (D&C 82:11–15)

In book 1, we learned that Zion was our origin and will be our destiny. She is our ideal, and she is also the antithesis of Babylon. Zion is the standard among celestial and celestial-seeking people.[2] Joseph Smith declared that the establishment of Zion should be our greatest desire: "We ought to have the building up of Zion as our greatest object."[3] Brigham Young taught that "[Zion] commences in the heart of each person."[4] Clearly, the responsibility to become a Zion people rests upon each of us individually. Our obligation is to accept every revealed Zion principle and put it into practice.

That obligation begins with formally accepting the Atonement of Jesus Christ by receiving the new and everlasting covenant. Widely misunderstood, this covenant is the *umbrella covenant* under which all other gospel covenants exist. The new and everlasting covenant is not only the product of the Atonement, but it is the vehicle by which we can access the Atonement's power to save and exalt us.

The new and everlasting covenant, along with its supporting covenants, serves to cleanse us, separate us from the world, prepare us for coronation, and protect us from Satan. These covenants endow us with keys to the knowledge and power of God, and they establish us in our eternal kingdoms. Collectively, these covenants and the laws of God are enveloped by the new and everlasting covenant.[5] This Covenant is also a contract,

---

1 D&C 42:67.
2 D&C 105:5.
3 Smith, *Teachings of the Prophet Joseph Smith*, 60.
4 Young, *Discourses of Brigham Young*, 118.
5 McConkie, *Mormon Doctrine*, 529–30.

which, remarkably, is agreed to by each member of the Godhead: the Father, the Son, and the Holy Ghost—a contract which is described as a marriage, the most intimate of relationships. Love is the single most motivating factor of the Covenant.

To become Zion people and thus ensure our salvation and exaltation, we must enter into the new and everlasting covenant and abide in it forevermore. By this, we witness that we have made a choice between Zion and Babylon. Furthermore, we witness that we agree to follow the Covenant to its perfect conclusion: to snatch us from Babylon, to single us out, to purify and sanctify our hearts, to prepare us in every way to regain the presence of God, and to obtain our inheritance and our crown. "This is Zion: THE PURE IN HEART."[6]

---

[6] D&C 97:21.

Section 1
Preface to the New and Everlasting Covenant

On January 2, 1831, the Lord promised the Prophet Joseph Smith that he would reveal to him "the law," which was the law of Zion, that would open the door to an endowment of "power from on high."[7] In obedience to the Lord's commandment, the Prophet traveled to Kirtland, Ohio, and on February 9, 1831, he received the "law of the Church," known as section 42 of the Doctrine and Covenants. Within that revelation, the Lord promised to reveal "church covenants, such as shall be sufficient to establish you, both here and in the New Jerusalem."[8] That is, the Lord was going to reveal to the Prophet the foundational covenants and laws of Zion. Significantly, the cross references for Doctrine and Covenants 42:67 lead to:

1. The New and Everlasting Covenant. (D&C 132:4–7)
2. The Oath and Covenant of the Priesthood. (D&C 84:33–44)
3. The Law of Consecration. (D&C 82:11–15)

These three covenants, recently mentioned in the introduction, are the Pillars of Zion that arise from the foundation of the Atonement. Because all gospel covenants and laws are included in the new and everlasting covenant, we will examine this covenant first.

Perhaps no discovery is more astonishing or humbling than the realization that the Father, the Son, and the Holy Ghost have invited us to become *one* with them. To be beckoned into their inner circle and to be offered all that they have and the chance to become all that they are constitutes unparalleled blessings that speak to their generosity and love. In his address entitled "The New and Everlasting Covenant," BYU professor Chauncey C. Riddle explained: "To be invited to join them by hearing the gospel of Jesus Christ is to receive *the greatest message in the universe*; to be enabled to join them by re-

---

[7] D&C 38:32.
[8] D&C 42:67.

ceiving the new and everlasting covenant is to have *the greatest opportunity in the universe;* to be joined with them is *the greatest gift in the universe,* which gift is life eternal, sharing with them all the good they have and are (D&C 14:7)."[9]

Perhaps equally humbling is the realization that their primary purpose for doing all that they do is to offer us the greatest degree of happiness.

The Plan of Happiness

The plan of happiness is central to becoming a Zion person. Happiness is always associated with Zion: "and surely there could not be a happier people among all the people who had been created by the hand of God."[10] The end purpose of our creation is happiness: "men are that they might have joy."[11] The ultimate definition of happiness is to be like God; the more we approach the stature of God in attributes, knowledge, power, and dominion, the happier we are. Conversely, the definition of misery is to be like Satan. Misery is always associated with Babylon.

To become like God and experience his level of happiness rests on two criteria: (1) Justice—the system of celestial laws that make God who he is and provide him what he has; that is, God's power and quality of life derive from his obedience to celestial laws. (2) Mercy—the Lord's love, grace, forbearance, clemency, and pity on us lesser beings, as he patiently works with us to help us to become like him. To a great extent our happiness depends upon God's merciful interaction with us and our extending mercy to others.[12]

The Covenant of the Gods

In a premortal council of the Gods[13] (which preceded the Council in Heaven we attended), the Father, the Son, and the Holy Ghost entered into a covenant to work together for the happiness, salvation, and exaltation of the Father's children. Joseph Smith taught that an "everlasting covenant was made between three personages before the organization of this earth, and relates to their dispensation of things to men on the earth; these personages, according to Abraham's record, are called God the first, the Creator; God the second, the Redeemer; and God the third, the witness or Testator."[14] Our interaction with these three Gods began before the world was created, continues here, and will endure into eternity. Every aspect of our interaction with them has to do with our present redemption and our eternal happiness.

Too often we miss the fact that the Father, the Son, and the Holy Ghost define their dealings with us in terms of *relationship.* Each one of us is dearer to them than we can comprehend. Motivated solely by their relationship with us, they initiated the plan of happiness.[15]

---

9   Riddle, "The New and Everlasting Covenant," 224–25; emphasis added.
10 4 Nephi 1:16.
11 2 Nephi 2:25.
12 See Alma 42:15.
13 Smith, *Teachings of the Prophet Joseph Smith,* 349.
14 Smith, *Teachings of the Prophet Joseph Smith,* 190.
15 Alma 42:1–26.

In the premortal world, when the Father announced the plan of happiness, we shouted for joy, perhaps because the plan's far-reaching benefits were so extraordinary.[16] In that supreme act of love, Heavenly Father offered us the opportunity to become what he is. He held nothing back. His package included indivisible access to and inheritance of the totality of his kingdom, the fulness of his power, the keys to the library of everything he knows, and the ability to become like him in perfections, characteristics, and attributes. His offer included the quintessential gift of a physical body—a tabernacle of flesh and bones for our immortal spirits to eternally "act upon."[17] He also offered us the invaluable gift of divine education: the opportunity to experience good and evil and the unrestricted gift of agency to choose between them. Finally, he offered us the opportunity to enjoy his lifestyle—*eternal marriage and family*—with the promise of eternal posterity.[18]

Happiness Encompasses All That Is Good

Clearly, the plan of happiness offered us all that was *good*, which is called *righteousness*. Righteousness, according to Chauncey Riddle, is "that necessary order of social relationships in which beings of knowledge and power must bind themselves in order to live together in accomplishment and happiness for eternity."[19] Happiness is wholly dependent upon righteousness, and it is in righteousness that Zion people weld themselves together by solemn covenants so that they become "predictable, dependable, and united so that they can be trusted. They bind themselves to be honest, true, chaste, and benevolent so that they can do good for all other beings, which good they do by personal sacrifice to fulfill all righteousness."[20] Thus, being and doing *good* and being and doing *righteousness* are synonymous terms; *goodness* and *righteousness* are unifying, perfecting, selfless principles that produce happiness. On the other hand, *evil*, the opposite of *goodness* and *righteousness*, is without discipline, a law unto itself,[21] a corrupting and self-serving principle that produces misery. Evil defines Babylon.

Heavenly Father structured the plan of happiness so as to mercifully wrest us from Babylon, from our complacency, from our evil tendencies, and from the effects of the Fall. Heavenly Father built into the plan of happiness his promise that he would endow us with the Light of Christ, which is an agent employed by the Holy Ghost to "feel after"[22] us and draw us out of Babylon and into Zion. By means of that light, the Holy Ghost would continually offer us opportunities to view ourselves in our "awful state,"[23] for the purpose of shaking us loose from Babylon. Moreover, the Father promised that he would offer each of us an unmistakable witness of the truth by the power of the Holy Ghost, so that we might reconsider our destructive path, repent of evil, and embrace "the godly order of good."[24] Clearly, the Father makes every effort to offer us happiness.

---

16 Job 38:7.
17 2 Nephi 2:13–14.
18 D&C 132:24, 55.
19 Riddle, "The New and Everlasting Covenant," 225.
20 Riddle, "The New and Everlasting Covenant," 225.
21 D&C 88:21–35.
22 D&C 112:13.
23 Ether 4:15.
24 Riddle, "The New and Everlasting Covenant," 225.

Balancing Justice and Mercy

To make the plan of happiness operational, the Father first instigated the covenant of justice,[25] that system of laws he obeyed in order to become who he is and enjoy what he has. That is, by obedience to celestial law he was justified to enjoy the blessings associated with those laws. By living those laws, we, God's children, can progress and become like him in every way. That is the process that leads to true happiness.

Knowing that his children would break the celestial laws while they struggled to assimilate them in their lives, and knowing that those broken laws would consign his children "forever to be cut off from his presence,"[26] the Father decreed a second law, which would have the power to override the consequences of broken celestial laws and to thereby save his children. That new law is called the covenant of mercy.[27] We know this law by another name: the new and everlasting covenant.

The covenant of mercy called for the Father to provide an atoning Savior to balance the demands of justice against the purposes of mercy: "And now, the plan of mercy could not be brought about except an atonement should be made; therefore God himself [Jesus Christ] atoneth for the sins of the world, to bring about the plan of mercy, to appease the demands of justice, that God might be a perfect, just God, and a merciful God also."[28] Mercy would also allow the children of God to receive physical bodies like their Father's, with the assurance that these eternal gifts would not be cancelled out by death. The Savior's merciful universal Resurrection would make that possible.[29]

Accessing the benefits of mercy through the Atonement was decreed to be a matter of individual choice. To facilitate that choice, the Father instigated a covenant that we could choose to embrace if we desired to access the Atonement, draw upon its mercy, receive shelter from the demands of justice, and be placed beyond the reach of our enemies. This covenant is called the new and everlasting covenant, and we enter it by our individual agency.

Placed beyond Our Enemies

The Atonement makes goodness, righteousness, happiness, and salvation possible. According to Joseph Smith, salvation is the power to be placed beyond the reach of one's enemies.[30] The specific enemy he spoke of was death, but, as Brother Riddle says, "The great enemy of each human being is himself, for in our weakness and selfishness we are and do evil."[31] We, alone, can neither save ourselves nor fully overcome our weakness or selfishness.

Overcoming our natural selves and our enemies is made possible "only if we fully cooperate with Jesus Christ."[32] He has the ability to cleanse us completely of the stains

---

25 Alma 42:13–15.
26 Alma 42:14.
27 See Alma 42:13–15.
28 Alma 42:15.
29 See Alma 11:44.
30 Smith, *Teachings of the Prophet Joseph Smith*, 305.
31 Acts 4:12.
32 Riddle, "The New and Everlasting Covenant," 225–26.

of our evildoing and to transform us into righteous individuals who have no more desires to do evil.[33] This process leads to progressively higher levels of happiness. By entering into the new and everlasting covenant for the purpose of accepting the Atonement of Jesus Christ, a repentant person can be "rescued from being and doing evil" through the "merits and mercy of the Son of God."[34]

How Mercy Appeases Justice

That mercy is a covenant is an essential truth. Every covenant or law of God is obeyed or disobeyed by individual choice. Specific blessings and consequences are associated with that choice, and either misery or happiness results. If we desire mercy, we must live the covenant associated with mercy. As we have learned, that covenant is the new and everlasting covenant, which we are required to receive in order to accept Jesus Christ and his Atonement. It is a truth that this Covenant springs from the Atonement and is the instrument by which we are justified to receive the Lord's mercy and by which the plan of happiness is realized.

Clearly, the new and everlasting covenant activates the plan of redemption. By means of this Covenant, the Father's children can receive celestial laws and experiment with them without being destroyed by them. By means of the Covenant, the children of God can lay hold on the blessings of the Atonement by choosing to repent, progress, obtain salvation, become like God, and inherit all that he has. This is the ultimate condition of Zion people. The new and everlasting covenant also sets us on the defined path that leads to eternal life, gives us the authority of God, places in our hands the *keys* (not priesthood administrative keys) to God's knowledge and power, and sets us up in our individual eternal kingdoms. Only the Atonement itself exceeds in glory the magnificence of the new and everlasting covenant. The two are inseparable, and both answer the end purpose of the Father's plan of mercy: *our happiness.*

Experiencing Contrasts Leads to Happiness

To lay hold on the plan of happiness, we must be presented with two contrasting revelations: (1) God and his goodness, and (2) our fallen situation. Because agency is crucial, the Lord uses contrast to motivate us to choose between these opposites.

As we have noted, there are good and bad consequences attached to God's laws. Breaking his commandments always results in being "cut off both temporally and spiritually from the presence of the Lord."[35] This is misery, which Alma described as "the gall of bitterness," and being "encircled about by the everlasting chains of death."[36] On the other hand, happiness always results from being brought, through our obedience, into

---

33 Alma 19:33.
34 Riddle, "The New and Everlasting Covenant," 225.
35 Alma 42:7.
36 Alma 36:18.

"the marvelous light of God."[37] For instance, after Alma had been "racked with eternal torment" for his sins and "harrowed to the greatest degree,"[38] he appealed to the Savior and suddenly swung from misery to happiness. He moved from "inexpressible horror" to "exquisite and sweet"[39] joy, from the "pains of a damned soul" to experiencing redemption and seeing "God sitting upon his throne, surrounded with numberless concourses of angels," with his soul longing to be there.[40] He exulted, "Oh, what joy, and what marvelous light I did behold." Then, describing the contrast, he added, "My soul was filled with joy as exceeding as was my pain."[41]

Clearly, seeing the contrast between good and evil motivates us toward happiness. After the Lord appeared to Moses, he left him to himself, and he was tempted by Satan. That contrast allowed Moses to experience the distinct difference between having the Lord and not having the Lord with him: "Now, for this cause I know that man is nothing, which thing I never had supposed." Moses also perceived the contrasting differences in glory between the Lord and Satan: "Moses looked upon Satan and said: . . . where is thy glory that I should worship thee?"[42] Now that Moses had experienced these contrasting visions, he was empowered to choose between misery and happiness. He said, "Depart from me, Satan, for this one God only will I worship, which is the God of glory."[43]

Similarly, but in reverse order, King Benjamin's people literally collapsed when they "viewed themselves in their own carnal state, even less than the dust of the earth." Then, after they cried out to the Lord for mercy, "the Spirit of the Lord came upon them, and they were filled with joy, having received a remission of their sins, and having peace of conscience."[44] Happiness came only after they experienced the contrast.

Similarly, and in a unique way, the Lord will offer us happiness by helping us understand who he is and showing us who and where we are. Then we, like King Benjamin's people, might be so astonished that we cry out for mercy and deliverance. Hopefully, when we are offered deliverance, we will choose to embrace it with all our hearts. The account of King Benjamin and his people teaches us the truth that mercy, deliverance, and eternal happiness are available to us only through the new and everlasting covenant. We note that King Benjamin's people were willing "to enter into a covenant with [their] God to do his will, and to be obedient to his commandments in all things that he [would] command [them], all the remainder of [their] days."[45]

Covenant-making leads to deliverance, which leads to happiness. After we have made a covenant and experienced deliverance and happiness, we will never want to return to our miserable past. Our desire now centers on the Lord sending the Holy Ghost to transform us into new creatures with new hearts. Because that process is beyond our ability, we look to Christ. To achieve a change of heart, we must first

---

37 Mosiah 27:29.
38 Alma 36:12.
39 Alma 36:14, 21.
40 Alma 36:16, 19–22.
41 Alma 36:20.
42 Moses 1:10, 13.
43 Moses 1:20.
44 Mosiah 4:12–13.
45 Mosiah 5:5.

accept Jesus Christ and his Atonement, enter into a covenant of salvation with him, and cooperate with him to the fullest extent.[46] Moreover, we must fully submit to his incomparable power and trust him as he remakes us into new creatures by planting the seeds of salvation and happiness in our souls.[47] "Thus human beings may become good and may become gods."[48]

To summarize, the Father, the Son, and the Holy Ghost entered into a premortal covenant to save and exalt the Father's children. A primary purpose of that covenant was that the children achieve ultimate happiness. Therefore, the Gods initiated the plan of happiness, which called for the Father to reveal the system of celestial laws that made him who he is and gave him what he has. The Gods knew that in the process of our learning those laws, we, God's children, would inevitably break the laws and become liable to pay severe penalties. Therefore, to mitigate the adverse effects of broken laws, the Gods initiated the plan of redemption, or the plan of mercy. That plan called for the Father to provide a Savior to rescue us from death and to atone for the consequences of broken celestial laws. The blessings of mercy through this plan could be accessed only by law and by choice; therefore, the Father established the new and everlasting covenant. Now his children could agree to obey this new law that would provide mercy, and God in turn would agree to set aside "the demands of justice."[49] Thus, justice could be satisfied, mercy could rescue and claim her own, and the children of God could progress in the Covenant until they achieved salvation, exaltation, and ultimate happiness, as the Gods had planned in the beginning.

Overview of the New and Everlasting Covenant

The new and everlasting covenant consists of two primary covenants: the covenant of baptism, and the oath and covenant of the priesthood.

The fulness of the priesthood covenant comes through (1) ordination for worthy men; (2) temple covenants and ordinances for worthy men and women; and (3) the temple sealing covenant, which is called the covenant of exaltation,[50] for worthy men and women.

Combined, the new and everlasting covenant and its supporting covenants serve to cleanse us, separate us from the world, prepare us for coronation, and protect us from Satan. They endow us with keys to the knowledge and power of God, and they establish us in our eternal kingdoms. Collectively, these covenants and the laws of God embrace the

---

46 2 Nephi 25:28.
47 2 Corinthians 5:17.
48 Riddle, "The New and Everlasting Covenant," 226.
49 Alma 42:15.
50 See Nelson, *The Power within Us*, 136; Smith, *Doctrines of Salvation*, 2:58. Note: Elder McConkie stated that men make a covenant of exaltation twice—once upon ordination to the Melchizedek Priesthood and again at the time of the marriage sealing. "Ordination to office in the Melchizedek priesthood and entering into that 'order of the priesthood' named 'the new and everlasting covenant of marriage' are both occasions when men make the covenant of exaltation, being promised through their faithfulness all that the Father hath (D&C 131:1–4; 84:39–41; 132; Num. 25:13)." (*Mormon Doctrine*, 167.)

new and everlasting covenant.[51] When we enter into the new and everlasting covenant, the Atonement satisfies the demands of justice that we cannot pay and encircles us in mercy's "arms of safety."[52]

The Covenant of Justice

Let us examine in depth the covenants of justice and mercy.

As we learned, the covenant of justice grew out of the premortal covenant of the Gods to provide the Father's children with consummate happiness. That could not happen unless the children were presented with the laws that the Father had obeyed that resulted in his exalted status. Therefore, to fulfill that premortal covenant, the Father revealed to us the pattern of his lifestyle, which pattern allows him to be both perfect and perfectly *just*. This pattern consists of obeying the immutable laws that govern him and all celestial beings. The purpose of the Father's revelation of these laws was to provide us the roadmap to follow to become just in the way that the Father is just. This purpose is central to the covenant of justice. Joseph Smith taught that "God Himself found Himself in the midst of spirits and glory. Because He was greater He saw proper to institute laws whereby the rest, who were less in intelligence, could have a privilege to advance like Himself and be exalted with Him, so that they might have one glory upon another in all that knowledge, power, and glory. So He took in hand to save the world of spirits."[53]

To that end, the Father decreed a single *umbrella law* that would govern all other laws: "There is *a law*, irrevocably decreed in heaven before the foundations of this world, upon which all blessings are predicated."[54] That is, atop the covenant of justice stands the supreme umbrella law, under which *every other* law of God exists; each of God's laws must be comprised of two things: immutable blessings ("when we obtain any blessing from God, it is by obedience to that law upon which it is predicated"[55]), and immutable punishments ("all mankind . . . were in the grasp of justice . . . which consigned them forever to be cut off from his presence"[56]).

Who Are the Just, and How Are They Justified?

We read of an early manifestation of the covenant of justice, including its blessings and punishments, when the Gods stated their purpose for creating the world: "And we will prove them herewith, to see if they will do all things whatsoever the Lord their God shall command them; and they who keep their first estate shall be added upon; and they who keep not their first estate shall not have glory in the same kingdom with those who keep their first estate; and they who keep their second estate shall have glory added upon their

---

51   McConkie, *Mormon Doctrine*, 529–30.
52   Alma 34:16.
53   Larson, "The King Follett Discourse," 204.
54   D&C 130:20.
55   D&C 130:21.
56   D&C 1:31.

heads for ever and ever."⁵⁷ Those who keep their second estate and receive eternal glory are called "the just," an appellation that seems to suggest that they are in the process of being fashioned in the similitude of God, who is fully just. They are those who: (1) have been "faithful in the testimony of Jesus while they lived in mortality," (2) have "offered sacrifice in the similitude of the great sacrifice of the Son of God," and (3) have "suffered tribulation in their Redeemer's name."⁵⁸ That is, faithfulness, willingness to sacrifice, and suffering tribulation while remaining true describe the just. Clearly, those who are "just" *chose* to become just by obeying celestial laws in the same way God obeyed them. Therefore, according to the covenant of justice, they are *justified* in receiving the blessings associated with obeyed laws.

The Lord describes the just and their blessings this way:

> They are they who received the testimony of Jesus, and believed on his name and were baptized after the manner of his burial, being buried in the water in his name, and this according to the commandment which he has given—
>
> That by keeping the commandments they might be washed and cleansed from all their sins, and receive the Holy Spirit by the laying on of the hands of him who is ordained and sealed unto this power;
>
> And who overcome by faith, and are sealed by the Holy Spirit of promise, which the Father sheds forth upon all those who are just and true.
>
> They are they who are the church of the Firstborn.
>
> They are they into whose hands the Father has given all things—
>
> They are they who are priests and kings, who have received of his fulness, and of his glory;
>
> And are priests of the Most High, after the order of Melchizedek, which was after the order of Enoch, which was after the order of the Only Begotten Son.
>
> Wherefore, as it is written, they are gods, even the sons of God—
>
> Wherefore, all things are theirs, whether life or death, or things present, or things to come, all are theirs and they are Christ's, and Christ is God's.
>
> And they shall overcome all things.
>
> Wherefore, let no man glory in man, but rather let him glory in God, who shall subdue all enemies under his feet.

---

57 Abraham 3:25–26.
58 D&C 138:12–13.

These shall dwell in the presence of God and his Christ forever and ever.

These are they whom he shall bring with him, when he shall come in the clouds of heaven to reign on the earth over his people.

These are they who shall have part in the first resurrection.

These are they who shall come forth in the resurrection of the just.

These are they who are come unto Mount Zion, and unto the city of the living God, the heavenly place, the holiest of all.

These are they who have come to an innumerable company of angels, to the general assembly and church of Enoch, and of the Firstborn.

These are they whose names are written in heaven, where God and Christ are the judge of all.

These are they who are just men made perfect through Jesus the mediator of the new covenant, who wrought out this perfect atonement through the shedding of his own blood.

These are they whose bodies are celestial, whose glory is that of the sun, even the glory of God, the highest of all, whose glory the sun of the firmament is written of as being typical.[59]

Justification and Agency

The covenant of justice could not function without agency. It was to be by choice that we could become just and justified for the highest blessings. Our choice would translate into obedience to God's laws, which we would be required to obey by sacrifice.[60] That is, in the process of obeying a law, we are always faced with alternatives, and thus we must sacrifice all other choices in favor of choosing one course of action. Thus it was determined in the beginning that obedience to God's laws would be proven by sacrifice, and that the combination of obedience and sacrifice would justify us for blessings. That is, we would be exalted in proportion to our obedience and sacrifice. Let us note here that we are attempting to explore the law of justice more deeply than is typically understood.

The Fall became the perfect environment in which obedience and sacrifice could be best demonstrated. Clearly, to choose to obey by sacrifice without memory of our premortal existence with Heavenly Father defines the desires of heart. The Fall provided

---

59   D&C 76:51–70.
60   D&C 97:8.

Section 1   Preface to the New and Everlasting Covenant

an atmosphere in which each person could "see for himself if he [would] choose good or evil."[61] Here in mortality it is decided once and for all if we can be forever trusted with the Father's unlimited knowledge and power.

Brother Riddle explains the covenant of justice this way:

> The conditions of the first covenant, the covenant of justice, were these: 1. Father would give his children instruction and commandments. 2. Any child who would believe Father and obey his every commandment, without exception, would in that obedience grow to attain and maintain all the good that Father is and does, which is exaltation. 3. Any child who disobeyed any single commandment of Father, would, without exception, immediately die spiritually, which spiritual death is to be cut off from Father's presence, no longer to be able to grow in his order of good (Alma 42:14). 4. For every transgression of a commandment of Father, the offender must suffer for that sin and make full restitution for that sin, this suffering and restitution being at least equal to the suffering and loss caused to the person(s) against whom the transgression was committed (Alma 42:22–28).[62]

Why is justice termed a *covenant* here? Because every person who desired to progress and become like God had to agree that: (1) God is the supreme lawgiver; (2) his laws are just; and (3) we would accept the consequences of his laws, which would either qualify us for immutable blessings or condemn us to eternal punishments. Perhaps a reason why Satan's followers were cast out of heaven[63] was that they refused to enter into the covenant of justice. When they rejected God and his covenant, they suffered the law's eternal consequences. The important point is this: Each one of us voluntarily entered into the covenant of justice and agreed to its terms; otherwise we would not be here. This was the covenant by which we gained a physical body, earned the privilege of experiencing mortality, and received the opportunity to choose eternal life and exaltation.

Celestial Law

The covenant of justice is comprised of laws that qualify us for celestial glory. Often stated in the singular, these laws are called the *Celestial Law*, the *Law of Christ*, the *Law of the Celestial Kingdom*, or the *Law of the Gospel*. The celestial law, according to Elder McConkie, is "that law by obedience to which men gain an inheritance in the

---

61   Riddle, "The New and Everlasting Covenant," 227.
62   Riddle, "The New and Everlasting Covenant," 228.
63   See Moses 4:1–2; Revelation 12:7–11.

Kingdom of God. . . . It is the law of the gospel [that] qualifies men for admission to the Celestial Kingdom."[64] "And they who are not sanctified through the law which I have given unto you, even the *law of Christ* [or the celestial law], must inherit another kingdom, even that of a terrestrial kingdom, or that of a telestial kingdom. For he who is not able to abide the law of a celestial kingdom cannot abide a celestial glory."[65] Elder McConkie ties the celestial law or the law of Christ, to Zion people: "Those who have the companionship of the Holy Ghost and are guided thereby in their lives are 'able to abide the law of a Celestial Kingdom,' including the Law of Consecration or anything else the Lord might ask of them. They are the ones who—'united according to the union required by the law of the celestial kingdom' (D&C 105:1–5)—will build up Zion in the last days."[66]

If we desire to achieve the celestial kingdom, we must set our sights higher than the telestial world in which we live; we must look beyond the telestial laws that govern such a world. That is not easy. Whenever we encounter any celestial law, we are hard-pressed to explain it. We often suffer culture shock when something celestial is manifested in our telestial environment.

God's celestial laws do not make much sense here. For instance, how can God travel at the speed of *thought* when science claims that nothing can exceed the speed of light? Or how can God know every detail of the future as if he were viewing it in present time? Or how is he able to be with each person individually when there are billions of us pleading for his attention at any given moment? The questions continue. For instance, how could water sustain the weight of a man and allow him to walk upon it as though it were solid pavement? And, speaking of water, how could it be instantly transformed into wine that had the taste of vintage aging? Moreover, how could a few fishes and loaves of bread feed thousands *until they were filled* and the quantity of the remnants exceed the original resource? How could the resurrected Savior invite some twenty-five hundred people to step forward one by one and touch his wounds, then organize the Apostles, teach major sermons, instruct the people on prayer, explain his mission concerning the entire house of Israel, prophesy, invite all twenty-five hundred to come to him again and this time bring their sick to be healed, then pray for the people, bless the children with angelic ministrations, instruct them concerning the sacrament, give the Apostles power to confer the Holy Ghost—*and do this during the daylight hours of a single day?*[67] Or, on a more personal basis, how can a newly ordained elder become the agent of healing by simply speaking words? How can paying 10 percent result in an amount greater than the original principal? How can the consecration of time, talents, and resources result in prosperity rather than poverty? Clearly, celestial laws are foreign here, but, nevertheless, we must embrace them if we ever hope to become Zion people.

---

64   McConkie, *Mormon Doctrine*, 117.
65   D&C 88:21–22; emphasis added.
66   McConkie, *Mormon Doctrine*, 117.
67   3 Nephi 12–17.

Preserved, Perfected, and Sanctified by the Laws of God

Flight is a complicated process wholly dependent upon adherence to the laws of aerodynamics. By obeying these laws, gravitation works for us rather than against us. To achieve flight, the wing of a plane must be thick and rounded on the upper surface and flat on the lower surface. Thus, the air that flows over the wing accelerates and becomes thinner than the air that flows under the wing. The difference in air density over and under the wing gives the airplane lift. The aircraft suddenly becomes buoyant like a boat floating on water; it is as though the plane is floating on air. Without interrupting the laws of gravitation, volume, mass, and velocity, but rather by applying them and causing them to work together, flight becomes possible.

So it is with the celestial laws of God. Obeyed, they result in a level of safety, security, power, and exaltation that otherwise would not be achievable. Broken, they result in danger, instability, helplessness, and damnation. Renowned filmmaker Cecil B. DeMille said, "We cannot break the Ten Commandments. We can only break ourselves against them."[68]

The Lord revealed to Joseph Smith the power of obedience to the celestial law: "And again, verily I say unto you, *that which is governed by law is also preserved by law and perfected and sanctified by the same*. That which breaketh a law, and abideth not by law, but seeketh to become a law unto itself, and willeth to abide in sin, and altogether abideth in sin, cannot be sanctified by law, neither by mercy, justice, nor judgment. Therefore, they must remain filthy still."[69] If a person insists on becoming a law unto himself, he will earn the telestial kingdom, where he can never hope to be preserved by the celestial law. Prisons are filled with people who reject law, and cemeteries contain the remains of many who broke themselves against the laws.

With regard to obeying the celestial law, we have a choice: we can remain forever telestially earthbound, or we can apply the laws of celestial flight and soar. "All kingdoms have a law given," the Lord said. "And unto every kingdom is given a law; and unto every law there are certain bounds also and conditions. All beings who abide not in those conditions are not justified."[70] We cannot expect to live a telestial law and achieve celestial benefits. If the celestial kingdom is our goal, we must learn and embrace the celestial law. This law alone will *preserve, perfect, and sanctify* us in that exalted kingdom.

Blessed As If We Understood

Amazingly, our obeying a law that we do not fully understand will still result in our receiving that law's benefits. Without our fully comprehending the laws of aerodynamics, we are still willing to board airplanes and fly from one destination to another. Our faith is in the laws that make flight possible. We believe that they are constant and will not fail; therefore, most of us climb aboard planes in faith rather than by knowledge.

---

68 DeMille, *BYU Speeches of the Year*, May 31, 1957, 6.
69 D&C 88:34–35; emphasis added.
70 D&C 88:36, 38–39.

Our obeying celestial law "as a child, submissive, meek, humble, patient,"[71] results in our receiving the law's blessings *as if we fully understood*. Over time, as we have more experience with the laws of God, we receive more understanding and our faith is quickened; that understanding will increase until we know all that God knows. Until then we progress in the safety, and the preserving, perfecting, and sanctifying power of the celestial law, with faith that the purpose of the law is to make of us Saints "through the atonement of Jesus Christ."[72] The end purpose of celestial law, of course, is to make of us celestial people, who, by definition, are people of Zion.

The Covenant of Mercy

The Father knew that once we had a physical body and began to encounter good and evil, we would inevitably choose wrong. Broken laws of God carry severe consequences. In addition to specific penalties, the covenant of justice universally demands that each divine broken law carry the penalty of *spiritual death*,[73] the consequence that means we are cut off from God forever.[74] No more are we fit for the celestial kingdom; the condition of having or being in the presence of God is one of perfection: "Wherefore . . . all men, everywhere, must repent, or they can in nowise inherit the kingdom of God, for no unclean thing can dwell there, or dwell in his presence."[75] We immediately see the harshness of justice and the necessity of mercy. Because all of us have fallen short and are separated from God by the demands of justice, we are, and would be forever, subject to Satan, and therefore miserable, were it not for the Lord's merciful intervention.

So that we could learn from our mistakes without being destroyed by them, God established a second covenant, the covenant of mercy. From the beginning, the Father's plan determined that the Atonement would serve as the foundation of the covenant of mercy. Without the Atonement, our agency would prove irreparably fatal. "And thus we see that all mankind were fallen, and they were in the grasp of justice; yea, the justice of God, which consigned them forever to be cut off from his presence."[76]

According to professor Chauncey C. Riddle, the covenant of mercy is called the new and everlasting covenant. It is *new* "because it is the second covenant (see Moses 6:56)," meaning that it follows the first covenant, which is the covenant of justice.[77] The covenant of mercy is also new because it is "revealed *new*"[78] to each person who receives it. The covenant is everlasting in that "the gospel is the everlasting covenant because it is ordained by Him who is Everlasting and also because it is everlastingly the same."[79] If we obey the terms of the covenant of mercy (which will be explained later), we gain access to the Atonement, which has power to pay the price of our sins and encircle us in the arms of safety.[80]

---

71 Mosiah 3:19.
72 Mosiah 3:19.
73 2 Nephi 9:12.
74 Alma 42:14.
75 Moses 6:57.
76 Alma 42:14.
77 Riddle, "The New and Everlasting Covenant," 226, 228.
78 McConkie, *Mormon Doctrine,* 530; emphasis added.
79 McConkie, *Mormon Doctrine,* 529.
80 Alma 34:16.

Mercy and Grace

The Atonement provides us with the Savior's grace, or enabling power, so that we might grow and learn from our mistakes while we try to adopt the celestial laws as a way of life. We access the Atonement by the new and everlasting covenant. The Atonement rescues us from physical and spiritual death, the negative effects of the Fall, the demands of justice, and the chains of Satan. The merciful Atonement of Jesus Christ recompenses every wrong perpetrated upon or suffered by us, reconciles us to God, and transforms us into celestial beings. "And now, the plan of mercy could not be brought about except an atonement should be made; therefore God himself [Jesus Christ] atoneth for the sins of the world, to bring about the plan of mercy, to appease the demands of justice, that God [the Father] might be a perfect, just God, and a merciful God also."[81] By means of the Atonement of Jesus Christ and on the condition of repentance, every obstacle that stands between us and exaltation is eliminated.

By God's grace, mercy rehabilitates the sinner. Mercy does not call for us to recompense the Savior for his redeeming efforts; mercy does, however, ask that we repent and change so that we become more Christlike.[82]

Every person who has inhabited or will inhabit this earth chose the Father's plan over Satan's plan by accepting the Father's covenants of justice and mercy. Moreover, each member of the human race, from the worst to the best, covenanted in the premortal world to reject Satan and accept Jesus Christ as his or her personal Savior; otherwise we would not be here.[83] There was no other way to gain a physical body and receive the opportunity of mortality.

Justification

Within the new and everlasting covenant, the covenants of justice and mercy work hand in hand to make of us Zion people and propel us toward eternal life—to make us *just* or *justified*. We often think of justice in terms of inflicting penalties for sin, but justice also rewards us for obedience to God's eternal laws. Mercy assures that those rewards are given according to our best—not perfect—effort. As we have mentioned, this is a manifestation of *grace*—we do all that we can and Jesus Christ makes up the difference.[84] Thus, by obedience and grace, a child might be justified to receive the same reward for obedience as an apostle, as evidenced in the account of 3 Nephi, when both the children and the apostles were equally blessed with access to the Savior, his teachings, healing, and heavenly ministrations. Justification, therefore, means to be judged worthy of the blessings that are specified by the laws of God on the basis of our best efforts. In the end, of course, we understand that all blessings come to us by the merits of Jesus Christ.[85] We

---

81 Alma 42:15.
82 *Encyclopedia of Mormonism*, 776.
83 McConkie, *Mormon Doctrine*, 828.
84 Bible Dictionary, "Grace," 697.
85 2 Nephi 31:19; Moroni 6:4.

cannot obtain any blessing from God, become just, attain to Zion, or obtain inheritance in the celestial kingdom without being justified by obeying God's laws and by applying the grace that is available through the mercy of Jesus Christ.

The Holy Ghost is the Savior's *justifying* agent. Elder McConkie wrote: "What then is the law of justification? It is simply this: 'All covenants, contracts, bonds, obligations, oaths, vows, performances, connections, associations, or expectations' (D&C 132:7), in which men must abide to be saved and exalted, must be entered into and performed in righteousness so that the Holy Spirit can justify the candidate for salvation in what has been done. (1 Ne. 16:2; Jac. 2:13–14; Alma 41:15; D. & C. 98; 132:1, 62.) *An act that is justified by the Spirit is one that is sealed by the Holy Spirit of Promise, or in other words, ratified and approved by the Holy Ghost.*"[86]

Some of the most definitive statements on justification are found in the Sermon on the Mount and the sermon at the Nephite temple.[87] Brother Riddle says, "The Book of Mormon is the scripture that lays out with great clarity justification both as a process and a product [see Alma 5]."[88] Only by entering into the new and everlasting covenant can we exercise faith in Jesus Christ unto repentance, be cleansed from his sins through baptism, then live obediently by sacrifice so that the Holy Ghost can justify us to receive the prescribed blessings affixed to the laws of God. By this process, and by this only, can we truly become just.

Purification

Purification and *sanctification* are words that are often interchanged. That they are closely associated is evident. In this book, we will define *purification* as extracting any impurities that would stand between us and perfection; we will define *sanctification* as changing the purpose of something. (These will be explained more fully shortly.) We enter the new and everlasting covenant to draw upon the Atonement and become pure and therefore Zion-like.

Zion people are purified people; they are the "pure in heart."[89] Quoting Brother Riddle: "[The Atonement of Jesus Christ has the power to] reach into our bosom and give each of us a new heart."[90] Purification flows from the covenant of mercy; by covenant we agree to allow the Lord to extract from our lives all impurities and pollutions that would stand between us and the celestial kingdom. This is necessary because, ultimately, our desire to become Zion-like will require divine intervention: "To pour light and truth into the human vessel is not enough. As a child of Christ attempts to love the light and truth . . . each becomes aware of an alarming fact: having light and truth is no guarantee of being able to do what is right."[91] Only the Atonement can purify a heart.

---

86   McConkie, *Mormon Doctrine*, 408; emphasis added.
87   Matthew 5–7; 3 Nephi 12–14.
88   Riddle, "The New and Everlasting Covenant," 234.
89   D&C 97:21.
90   Riddle, "The New and Everlasting Covenant," 236.
91   Riddle, "The New and Everlasting Covenant," 236.

Purification is dependent upon two factors: (1) our complete effort to change and make amends, and (2) the grace of Jesus Christ to do for us what lies beyond our ability to do. The Savior is the Purifier, but the agent for the purification process is the Holy Ghost: "The Holy Ghost is also a purifier in that, because of Christ and the Atonement, this Spirit member of the Godhead has power given him to cleanse, sanctify, and purify the human soul (3 Ne. 27:19–21.)"[92] The process of purification is often called the baptism of fire.[93] We are fully immersed in the heat of the Lord's furnace to burn out of us all impurities. The Holy Ghost will persist in the process until he can commend us to God as being pure, that is, "true and faithful in all things" in the similitude of "Him whose very name is 'Faithful and True.'"[94]

We must do our part to purify ourselves, but in the end we will need the Holy Ghost and the Savior to make us completely pure. Brother Riddle said:

> If we have repented of every sin we can repent of, have made fourfold restitution as far as we are able [D&C 98:44; Luke 19:8], and have been reconciled to our brother [Matthew 5:23–24], we may present ourselves at the altar with a broken heart and a contrite spirit [2 Nephi 2:7] and plead in mighty prayer for this change of heart [Mormon 7:48; Mosiah 4:2]. Then and only then will our Savior reach in and give us a new heart. The new heart will be a pure heart, one that has no selfish desires, one that is willing to do the right thing. It will choose to do the will of God at all times and places, no matter what the opposition or the sacrifice involved.
>
> This new heart is made in the image of Jesus Christ, that same heart that enabled our Savior to say, "Father, not my will, but thine be done," that same heart that enabled him to live a sinless life, that same heart for which he was chosen to be the Firstborn and to be the Only Begotten. To be purified is to become literally a new creature in Christ, to die as to the old person that we were, literally to become of the heart and mind of [Christ]. The scriptures promise great rewards for those who qualify and take this step. The scriptural name for this new heart is "charity." Charity is to have a heart that loves with the pure love of Christ.[95]

---

92 McConkie, *Mormon Doctrine*, 612.
93 2 Nephi 31:13–14; D&C 20:41; 33:11; 39:6.
94 McConkie, *A New Witness for the Articles of Faith*, 316.
95 Riddle, "The New and Everlasting Covenant," 236–37.

Sanctification

Like purification, sanctification also flows from the covenant of mercy, which is the new and everlasting covenant. As much as we enter the Covenant to receive the blessings of the Atonement and become purified, we also enter the Covenant to be sanctified.

Sanctification is the *result* of being purified. When the contaminants, pollutions, and alloys have been burned from our souls, we emerge from the furnace sanctified; that is, we now have a new purpose. Let us examine, for example, the sacrament prayer, in which the priests bless and sanctify "profane" bread and, by the priesthood, change its purpose to calling us to remembrance of the body of Jesus Christ,[96] the Bread of Life.[97] Now blessed and sanctified (or "made holy"), the bread's purpose has changed from sustaining physical life to sustaining spiritual life. Likewise, a pile of stones can, by the priesthood, be changed in purpose to become an altar: "And thou shalt anoint the altar of the burnt offering, and all his vessels, and sanctify the altar: and it shall be an altar most holy."[98] Or a natural man can be purified of sin, then sanctified by the Holy Ghost, so that his purpose now becomes that of service to God: "And thou shalt put them upon Aaron thy brother, and his sons with him; and shalt anoint them, and consecrate them, and sanctify them, that they may minister unto me in the priest's office."[99]

The Savior sanctifies us through the Atonement, but the Holy Ghost is the agent of sanctification,[100] just as he is the agent of purification.[101] The Holy Ghost rids us of impurities so that he might change our purpose. This is purification and sanctification. We have a responsibility in receiving these blessings. We must actively participate in the process as the Savior and the Holy Ghost purify and sanctify us. The Lord commanded: "Sanctify yourselves; yea purify your hearts, and cleanse your hands and your feet before me, that I may make you clean."[102] None of this is possible outside the Covenant.

Our Responsibility

Our part of the sanctifying process requires that we separate ourselves from Babylon and all that is profane, unholy, and ungodly. To accomplish this, wrote *Mormon Times* editor Joseph A. Cannon, "We fast and pray, we 'wax stronger' in our humility and become 'firmer in the faith of Christ . . . even to the purifying and the sanctification of [our] hearts, which sanctification cometh because of [our] yielding [our] hearts unto God' (Helaman 3:35). If we 'come unto Christ' and 'deny [our]selves of all ungodliness' and yield our hearts to God, then we are 'sanctified in Christ by the grace of God through the shedding of the blood of Christ.' It is through this [process] that we can 'become holy

---

96 D&C 20:77.
97 John 6:35.
98 Exodus 40:10.
99 Exodus 28:41.
100 McConkie, *The Mortal Messiah*, 4:114.
101 Alma 13:11–12; 3 Nephi 27:19–21; D&C 84:33.
102 D&C 88:74.

[sanctified] without spot.' (Moroni 10:32–33)."[103] Thus each of us is commanded: "sanctify yourselves that your minds become single to God."[104]

Our effort to purify and sanctify ourselves begins with faith in Jesus Christ; we must believe that he has the power to cleanse and transform us, and we must trust in his methods and his timing. Faith in Jesus Christ—*true faith*—always leads to repentance; we must eliminate the impurities from our souls and change our purpose. Repentance leads to covenant-making; we desire to legitimize our resolve by entering into an agreement with the Lord for him to purify, sanctify, and make us in every way fit for the celestial kingdom. That agreement is called the new and everlasting covenant, and we enter that Covenant by the covenant of baptism. Now we are pronounced clean, but we are not yet pure and sanctified. For that reason, we receive a special gift: the gift of the consummate purifying and sanctifying agent, the Holy Ghost.[105]

Reception of the gift of the Holy Ghost is the baptism of fire spoken of in the scriptures.[106] When a person enters into the new and everlasting covenant, he does so for the purposes of receiving relief from his sins and starting down the path to becoming like God. That process of transformation requires burning out of him the impurities that made him a sinful "natural man,"[107] then molding him into a new creature,[108] a Saint,[109] to assume the image of God.[110]

The Crucible—The Baptism of Fire

A common metaphor for this sanctification process is the making of steel. When raw ore is placed in a crucible and heated in a furnace, the substance becomes molten and the properties separate. At that point, a skilled metallurgist can divide out the impurities from the pure, refined iron. An alloying process ensues, whereby the metallurgist carefully combines select elements in perfect proportion with the pure iron. The result is steel. But the process is not yet complete. For steel to become strong and not brittle, it must be subjected to reheating in the furnace, which is followed by pounding to align the molecules into their strongest position. The process of being thrust into the furnace and beaten is repeated multiple times until the steel is free from impurities and aligned so that it cannot be broken. At some point, the metallurgist pours the steel into a mold to change, or shape, it for its new purpose, and as a final step he polishes it. The finished product is incredibly strong and beautiful and it will remain so indefinitely.

In a similar manner, we are immersed in the crucibles attendant to the mortal experience, those fiery trials that heat, pound, mold, and polish us so that we might be purified, sanctified, and conformed to the image of God.[111] The Lord has every right to

---

103 Cannon, *Mormon Times,* June 12, 2008.
104 D&C 88:68.
105 2 Nephi 27:19–21.
106 See 2 Nephi 31:13–14; D&C 20:41; 33:11; 39:6.
107 Mosiah 3:19.
108 JST, 2 Corinthians 5:17.
109 Mosiah 3:19.
110 Alma 5:19.
111 Romans 8:29.

do this. We agreed to it when we entered into the new and everlasting covenant. John Taylor wrote: "I heard the Prophet Joseph say, in speaking to the Twelve on one occasion: 'You will have all kinds of trials to pass through. And it is quite as necessary for you to be tried as it was for Abraham and other men of God, and (said he) God will feel after you, and He will take hold of you and wrench your very heart strings, and if you cannot stand it you will not be fit for an inheritance in the Celestial Kingdom of God.'"[112]

Purified and Sanctified to Make an Offering

When we entered into the new and everlasting covenant, we agreed to submit to the Lord's crucible and allow him to make of us what we could not make of ourselves, and we also agreed to make an offering in righteousness. We read: "And he shall sit as a refiner and purifier of silver; and he shall purify the sons of Levi, and purge them as gold and silver, that they may offer unto the Lord an offering in righteousness."[113] We qualify as the sons of Levi. When we enter into the Melchizedek Priesthood, we become the sons of Aaron—who was the son of Levi—and the sons of Moses.[114] The offerings required of us are twofold: (1) a broken heart and a contrite spirit—"And ye shall offer for a sacrifice unto me a broken heart and a contrite spirit. And whoso cometh unto me with a broken heart and a contrite spirit, him will I baptize with fire and with the Holy Ghost"[115]—and (2) "a book containing the records of our dead."[116]

Job understood the process and submitted to the Lord's crucible: "When he hath tried me, I shall come forth as gold."[117] Sometimes this process is called trying, or chastisement, and we must endure it or forfeit our eternal inheritance: "My people must be tried in all things, that they may be prepared to receive the glory that I have for them, even the glory of Zion; and he that will not bear chastisement is not worthy of my kingdom."[118] Interestingly, the word *chastise* means more than to punish; it also means "to make chaste,"[119] or to purify. Job patiently endured the Lord's chastisement without murmuring. To murmur is to believe in God while simultaneously complaining about how he is managing the affairs of one's life. Job, by contrast, waited confidently on the Lord's deliverance from the crucible he was in. He followed the same admonition that Joseph Smith gave to the Saints: "Therefore, dearly beloved brethren, let us cheerfully do all things that lie in our power; and then may we stand still, with the utmost assurance, to see the salvation of God, and for his arm to be revealed."[120] Whereas murmuring postpones, or cancels out, blessings, cheerfully submitting in patience summons the Lord's deliverance.

Only the grace of Jesus Christ enables us to endure the heat of the purifying and sanctifying procedure while trusting him in the process. The Lord will strengthen us

---

112 Taylor, *Journal of Discourses,* 24:197.
113 3 Nephi 24:3; D&C 128:24.
114 D&C 84:31–34.
115 3 Nephi 9:20.
116 D&C 128:24.
117 Job 23:10.
118 D&C 136:31.
119 *Encyclopedia of Mormonism,* 264.
120 D&C 123:17.

and uphold us until we can make an offering unto him in righteousness, which offering brings us finally to where we desired to be someday when we entered into the new and everlasting covenant. Only the Lord's grace can expunge us of all impurities; only his grace can transform us and give us a new purpose. The promises to those who are purified and sanctified are unequalled: "And unto him that repenteth and sanctifieth himself before the Lord shall be given eternal life."[121]

Oneness or Unification

A significant goal of the new and everlasting covenant is to make us *one*—one with the Father, the Son, and the Holy Ghost, one with our spouse, one with our family, one with the children of Zion. Oneness and separation are opposites. Whereas separation causes misery, oneness, or unity, results in joy. The Atonement restores that which was lost and reunites that which was separated: "The literal meaning of the word 'Atonement' is self-evident: At-one-ment, the act of unifying or bringing together what has been separated and estranged."[122] In the Atonement, we can readily see the principle of *oneness* as a central feature of the covenant of mercy or the new and everlasting covenant. Zion people are "of one heart and one mind";[123] they are *one*.

The Atonement of Jesus Christ makes us whole, reconciled, and *one*. Alma referred to this condition of oneness as *restoration*.[124] Because the covenant of justice demands the separation of the sinner from God, because the condition of this telestial world is continual decay, deterioration, entropy, and corruption, and because physical death is the inevitable end of every mortal life form, the Father, in order to be just, established the plan of restoration as a manifestation of his mercy to restore everything to its proper order. Alma taught: "The plan of restoration is requisite with the justice of God; for it is requisite that all things should be restored to their proper order."[125] Furthermore, the Prophet Joseph Smith said, God glorifies himself "by saving [restoring] all that His hands had made, whether beasts, fowls, fishes or men."[126]

In gospel terms, *separation* is another term for *death*. The separation of a sinner from God is *spiritual death*; the separation of the physical body from the spirit is *physical death*. Our fallen condition is, by definition, a *death*, a separation from God that causes misery, and is, therefore, in need of the Lord's immediate attention and restoration: "All men that are in a state of nature, or I would say, in a carnal state, are in the gall of bitterness and in the bonds of iniquity; they are without God in the world, and they have gone contrary to the nature of God; therefore, they are in a state contrary to the nature of happiness."[127]

Death can take other forms. For example, husbands and wives can experience a kind of emotional death when they are separated by oppression, distance, time, lack

---

121 D&C 133:62.
122 *Encyclopedia of Mormonism*, 83.
123 Moses 7:18.
124 Alma 40–41.
125 Alma 41:2.
126 Smith, *Teachings of the Prophet Joseph Smith*, 291.
127 Alma 41:11.

of affection, indifference, neglect, abuse, unkind words, or physical death. Likewise, a type of death can be experienced in cases of the separation of children from parents, friends from friends, Saints from the Church, the gospel from the earth, people from their true identity and birthright, or individuals separated from their health, youth, innocence, rights, and possessions. When estrangement or breach occurs, misery almost inevitably follows, and it can feel like a death; but when all is restored, joy and peace ensue.

As we have said, restoration to oneness and unity is a central purpose of the At-one-ment. By the Atonement, the spirit becomes *at one* with the body; the husband and the wife become *at one* with each other; children become *at one* with their parents; friends become *at one* with each other; Saints become *at one* with the Church and its doctrines; individuals become *at one* with or restored to their health, youth, innocence, rights, and possessions, and we become *at one* with God and his children. How is this done? When we enter into the new and everlasting covenant, the Savior wraps us in his atoning mercy, which is the power to repair every breach, overcome every form of death, restore all that was lost to its perfect order, return us to God, and make us *one* with him. The power of the Atonement is to make all things *at one* and to seal them together in a form that can attain to perfection. In that condition, the creation can eventually achieve a fulness of joy. The Lord's restoration is complete and perfect: "And not one hair, neither mote, shall be lost, for it is the workmanship of mine hand."[128]

But we must beware: The law of restoration functions according to our actions and our desires. Alma taught:

> If their works were good in this life, and the desires of their hearts were good, . . . they should also, at the last day, be restored unto that which is good. And if their works are evil they shall be restored unto them for evil. Therefore, all things shall be restored to their proper order, . . . the one raised to happiness according to his desires of happiness, or good according to his desires of good; and the other to evil according to his desires of evil; for as he has desired to do evil all the day long even so shall he have his reward of evil when the night cometh. And so it is on the other hand. If he hath repented of his sins, and desired righteousness until the end of his days, even so he shall be rewarded unto righteousness. . . . For that which ye do send out shall return unto you again, and be restored.[129]

---

128 D&C 29:25.
129 Alma 41:3–6, 15.

Oneness and the Law of Restoration

The law of restoration follows natural laws. Amoeba are not restored as fish; fish are not restored as apes; apes are not restored as humans; and wicked individuals are not restored as righteous people: "And now behold, is the meaning of the word restoration to take a thing of a natural state and place it in an unnatural state, or to place it in a state opposite to its nature? O, my son, this is not the case; but the meaning of the word restoration is to bring back again evil for evil, or carnal for carnal, or devilish for devilish—good for that which is good; righteous for that which is righteous; just for that which is just; merciful for that which is merciful. . . . Do not suppose, because it has been spoken concerning restoration, that ye shall be restored from sin to happiness. Behold, I say unto you, wickedness never was happiness."[130]

What has this to do with becoming a Zion person? Zion is always described in terms of perfection, beauty, unity, and oneness; furthermore, Zion is described as a condition of no lack—things that have been divided from us are now restored, and we experience abundance. This is the condition of Zion people. The Atonement and the Covenant are always drawing us toward these ideals. Therefore, the more we align ourselves with the purifying, sanctifying, and unifying motions of the Atonement, and the more we abide in the Covenant, the more Zion-like we become; the more *at one* we become with God and his children.

Restoration and Resurrection

The law of restoration becomes operational when we enter into the new and everlasting covenant, and the law reaches its zenith in the Resurrection. Beyond being a victory over death and the eternal restoration of the body and spirit in "perfect form,"[131] the Resurrection is the consummate event wherein everything that we have lost or been denied by reason of the Fall is restored. Joseph Smith said, "All your losses will be made up to you in the resurrection, provided you continue faithful."[132] As much as the Fall renders us temporarily but significantly impotent, as compared with our former stature, and exposes us to evil and unclean spirits, pain, illness, hunger, aging, and other kinds of physical distress, the resurrection restores to us every loss that we have experienced and repairs each defeat. It is almost an understatement when we read that "the Lamb . . . shall feed them, and shall lead them unto living fountains of waters: and God shall wipe away all tears from their eyes."[133] To the degree that we have suffered or been opposed or denied, we shall be restored to happiness. In fact, the Lord promised that we would be restored *an hundredfold:* "And every one that hath forsaken houses, or brethren, or sisters, or father, or mother, or wife, or children, or lands, for my name's sake, shall receive *an hundredfold*, and shall inherit everlasting life."[134]

---

130 Alma 41:12–13, 10.
131 Alma 11:43–44; 40:23–26.
132 Smith, *Teachings of the Prophet Joseph Smith*, 296.
133 Revelation 7:17.
134 Matthew 19:29.

The scriptures state that resurrection is a free gift given to all through the grace and mercy of Jesus Christ,[135] but the quality of our resurrected glory is wholly dependent upon our works and desires.[136] For example, only celestial resurrection provides us a fulness of joy.[137] Only the eternal sealings of husbands to wives and children to parents can be fully realized in the Resurrection. Only celestial resurrection in the highest degree of glory provides righteous individuals the divine power of procreation.[138] Only celestial resurrection carries the possibility of exaltation, which includes obtaining the fulness of God's power and glory and receiving dominion over the angels.[139]

Brother Riddle said,

> Thus, after all probation has been extended, after each human creature has chosen the law by which he desires to be governed, after all things are set in order and there is no further need of the special change known as repentance, then our Savior extends the opportunity of resurrection to each human being through his priesthood order. Every soul will receive again a tabernacle of flesh and bone, nevermore to die. [Christ's] righteous children receive a tabernacle of *his own order*, a celestial body, having the same powers that he inherited from his Father in becoming the Only Begotten. Thus our Savior draws us into the same order of flesh and bone as that which he and Father enjoy.[140]

Joseph Smith taught that the Resurrection gives us power over all spirits;[141] it places us beyond all of our enemies and every opposition. Chauncey Riddle wrote: "Because of the circumstances in which Adam fell, he became subject to Satan, and that subjection would have been complete and final had not the Savior [provided the Atonement and Resurrection. But Jesus] by dying voluntarily . . . performed the sacrifice of the Atonement, *and by that sacrifice seized the keys of death and hell from Satan, who had gained them in the Fall*, and thus prepared the way for the resurrection of all mankind."[142] In other words, by the Atonement and by the Resurrection, Jesus Christ places us beyond the reach of our worst enemies, death and hell, and makes us free.

As noted above, although these descriptions appear on the surface to have little to do with Zion, they have everything to do with it. Zion is a condition of no lack and of abundance; it is beauty, perfection, and protection from enemies. Zion is the eternal

---

135 Alma 11:43–44.
136 Alma 41:3–5.
137 D&C 93:33–34; 138:17; D&C 93:33-34.
138 D&C 132:19.
139 D&C 132:20.
140 Riddle, "The New and Everlasting Covenant," 239.
141 Smith, *Teachings of the Prophet Joseph Smith*, 190; 2 Nephi 9:8.
142 Riddle, "The New and Everlasting Covenant," 237–38; emphasis added.

habitation of God. Zion people move toward this ideal in this life and fully realize it in the Resurrection. Then, they, as Zion people, remain as Zion people and abide in the celestial Zion society forever.

Hundredfold Restoration

As we have learned, the covenant of mercy called for an Atonement that would recompense our losses and afflictions "an hundredfold." The idea of a "hundredfold restoration" is repeated so often in the scriptures that we are obligated to give it consideration. For example, "But he shall receive an hundredfold now in this time, houses, and brethren, and sisters, and mothers, and children, and lands, . . . and in the world to come eternal life."[143] The Apostle Paul wrote, "Eye hath not seen, nor ear heard, neither have entered into the heart of man, the things which God hath prepared for them that love him."[144] Imagine experiencing the unjust loss of $10,000. The pain of that loss might be overwhelming. But suppose that the Lord were to restore to us $1,000,000. Suddenly, the $10,000 loss would fade away as a nonissue. We are redeemed by compensation that exceeds the debt—a hundredfold with the promise of an overabundance or perhaps an amount beyond measurement.

Or imagine this scenario: Let us say that we had committed a crime against another person, who sued us and received a $10,000 judgment, which we could not pay. Now, let us imagine that a benevolent friend stepped forward to rectify the situation by offering the offended person the $10,000, plus another $990,000 for damages. Could the offended person ever claim that he had not been treated justly? Clearly, the Lord's restoration is a manifestation of his mercy, "which overpowereth justice . . . and encircles them in the arms of safety, while he that exercises no faith unto repentance is exposed to the whole law of the demands of justice."[145] Clearly, in the Resurrection all losses and debts are restored to the extent that justice can never again make a claim—*an hundredfold!*

Oneness and Deliverance

At the heart of the Atonement are the issues of happiness, balancing justice and mercy, purifying and sanctifying us, justifying us for blessings based on the merits of Jesus Christ, bringing us into *oneness* with God and his children, and restoring us to a condition of perfection indicative of Zion. The Atonement allows us to become one in the Covenant, and oneness is made possible by redemption. What we do with that redemption determines whether or not we become Zion people. Unless we are drawn into unity, we are nothing and cannot fill the measure of our creation.[146]

Oneness, or unity, is characteristic of Zion, and thus of the celestial kingdom. There is inherent power in unity. Joseph Smith said, "The greatest temporal and spiritual

---
143 Mark 10:30.
144 1 Corinthians 2:9.
145 Alma 34:15–16.
146 D&C 49:17; 88:19, 25.

blessings which always come from faithfulness and concentrated effort, *never attended individual exertion or enterprise.*"[147] President Gordon B. Hinckley taught, "When you are united, your power is limitless. You can accomplish anything you wish to accomplish."[148] We become one and unified by covenant.

The Lord said, "I say unto you, be one; and if ye are not one ye are not mine."[149] Inasmuch as the Godhead are one,[150] so Zion people must likewise become one with each other and with the Father and with Jesus: "That they all may be one; as thou, Father, art in me, and I in thee, that they also may be one in us . . . ; that they may be one, even as we are one: I in them, and thou in me, that they may be made perfect in one."[151] We cannot fully accept the Atonement without becoming one with the Father and the Son and with each other by means of the Covenant. Whereas divisiveness is of the devil[152] and therefore characteristic of Babylon, *oneness* is of God and therefore characteristic of Zion: "And the Lord called his people ZION, because they were of one heart and one mind, and dwelt in righteousness; and there was no poor among them."[153]

Summary and Conclusion

In the premortal council of the Gods, the Father instituted the first covenant, called the covenant of justice, for the purpose of allowing his children the highest level of happiness. The purpose of the covenant of justice was to reveal the celestial laws by which the Father had become God, and by which his children could advance and become gods like him. Again, the terms of the covenant of justice are: (1) God is the supreme lawgiver; (2) his laws are just; and (3) all laws have immutable blessings and punishments that follow obedience and disobedience. Essential to the covenant of justice is agency; we rise or fall by personal choice. Agency was a central issue of the war in heaven. In that premortal setting, every person who has or would receive a physical body and thus have the potential to become like God chose to accept the covenant of justice.

The first covenant, the covenant of justice, was followed by the Father's establishing a second covenant: the covenant of mercy. The agent of mercy was Jesus Christ, and the vehicle of mercy was the Atonement. The way that we could begin to receive the purifying and sanctifying benefits of the Atonement was to enter into the new and everlasting covenant by the covenant and ordinance of baptism. Because the foundation of the covenant of mercy is the Atonement, and because key aspects of the Atonement are accessed by the new and everlasting covenant, the covenant of mercy and the new and everlasting covenant are synonymous.

---

147 Kimball, "Becoming the Pure in Heart," quoting Smith in *Teachings of the Prophet Joseph Smith,* 183; emphasis added.
148 Hinckley, "Your Greatest Challenge, Mother," 97.
149 D&C 38:27.
150 3 Nephi 11:36.
151 John 17:21–23.
152 3 Nephi 11:29.
153 Moses 7:18.

Section 1   Preface to the New and Everlasting Covenant

The covenant of mercy called for the Father to provide us a Savior to assure that the purposes of the covenant of justice, including the preservation of agency, justification for blessings or punishments, and advancement based on obedience, would remain intact. Moreover, the covenant of mercy provides that the demands of justice and the purposes of mercy can remain perfectly in balance so that God can be simultaneously just and merciful.[154] The covenant of mercy also provides a number of other blessings. For example, the merciful Atonement rescues us from the effects of the Fall and the consequences of our bad choices. Mercy also provides a means of payment of the debts for our sins, after our best efforts. Furthermore, the merciful Atonement allows the Holy Ghost to justify us to receive blessings for obeyed laws, even when we are not yet perfect.

By means of the Atonement and through the Holy Ghost, the covenant of mercy makes us just by progressively purifying our hearts; that is, the Holy Ghost expunges from us the impurities, contaminants, and pollutions that differentiate us from God and keep us from receiving his blessings. Similarly, the merciful Atonement allows the Holy Ghost to sanctify us; that is, to change our carnal, sensual, and devilish natures to the heart and nature of God. Finally, the merciful Atonement enacts the law of restoration and brings *oneness* where there has been loss or separation due to the Fall or transgression. Mercy restores everything in our lives to its perfect form—everything that has been lost by reason of separation or *death*, and makes *an hundredfold* recompense. Mercy, through the Atonement and by means of the new and everlasting covenant, makes us *one* with our true selves, with God, and with each other. This process of becoming *one* begins when we enter the covenant of mercy, or the new and everlasting covenant, and the process reaches its perfection in the Resurrection.

Central to the power of the merciful Atonement is the saving grace of Jesus Christ. We cannot rescue ourselves from the Fall or from the consequences of sin; make ourselves clean and purified so that we might be justified to receive blessings; make ourselves sanctified so that our nature and purpose changes; free ourselves from Satan's grasp; make ourselves one with God, our spouse, family, and the Saints of God; or, in terms of our approaching our ideal self, we become one in health, youth, and in eternal union of body and spirit—these things are totally beyond our capability without the Lord's grace. Such miraculous events are the work of God; we are completely dependent upon the Savior to accomplish these things in our behalf. His grace is that enabling power that allows us to do all that we can do with the faith that he will make up the difference where we fall short;[155] grace is the power that justifies imperfect beings to receive blessings that otherwise would be outside of our reach were it not for the merits of Jesus Christ.[156]

When we bind ourselves to Jesus Christ in the new and everlasting covenant, he assigns his agent, the Holy Ghost, to transform us into a god, like our Father. We cannot become truly righteous by our own efforts; we need the Lord's grace. Chauncey Riddle said:

---

154   Alma 42:13–15.
155   LDS Bible Dictionary, "Grace," 697.
156   Alma 24:10; Moroni 6:4.

> Only in him and by him are [we] able to do any good thing. The righteous acts [we] do are not strictly [our] own acts; therefore [we] take no credit for them. Rather do [we] give the glory to God. [We] know that [our] righteous acts are acts of Christ, chosen by the pure heart given by Christ, understood by the just mind given by Christ, carried out by the new strength given by Christ, redounding to the blessing of others in the priesthood might of Christ. Thus in Christ the righteous move, and live, and have their being (Acts 17:28). . . . When we endure to the end in the New and Everlasting Covenant, we will be literally transformed into the stature of Christ in heart, might, mind, and strength. . . . Thus the purpose of the new and everlasting covenant is to provide a means whereby every human being may come to be able to fulfill the first covenant [the covenant of justice].[157]

Now we understand what John meant when he said, "Beloved, now are we the sons of God, and it doth not yet appear what we shall be: but we know that, when he shall appear, we shall be like him; for we shall see him as he is."[158]

Such are the blessings of the covenant of mercy, the new and everlasting covenant, the magnificent plan that is founded on the Atonement and offered by the Father through his Only Begotten Son. This is the Covenant to which the Father, the Son, and the Holy Ghost effectively affix their names and place their godhood on the line to uphold, provided that we keep the terms of the Covenant. Truly, the new and everlasting covenant is the most glorious doctrine ever revealed. It contains the greatest hope and the most impressive promises of anything found on earth or in the far reaches of the universe. By abiding by its precepts, we can escape Babylon, flee to Zion, and forever abide safely in the embrace of our Eternal Father.

---

157 Riddle, "The New and Everlasting Covenant," 241–42.
158 1 John 3:2.

Section 2
The New and Everlasting Covenant
The First Pillar of Zion

Joseph Smith said, "For a man to be great, he must not dwell on small things."[159]

The first pillar of Zion is the New and Everlasting Covenant.[160] This Covenant is made possible by the Atonement of Jesus Christ and is the vehicle by which the Atonement becomes operative in our lives. Infinite and eternal in scope, the Covenant has the power to save men and women and transform them into the image of God. We are saved to the degree that we receive and conform to this Covenant. If we become complacent about the Covenant, we risk forfeiture of our privileges. Zion people build their lives upon the bedrock of the Atonement by entering into the new and everlasting covenant.

The new and everlasting covenant is the sum of all gospel covenants, ordinances, and commandments[161]—"the fulness of the gospel."[162] The purposes of entering into the Covenant are: (1) to obtain knowledge and power for personal salvation, and (2) to obtain knowledge and power to help save other people by teaching them of the Atonement and administering to them the Covenant.

God sets the terms of the Covenant and of every other saving covenant within the Covenant, and he invites us to accept those terms. Our *signature*, which signifies our agreement to the terms of the covenants, is the ordinance that is associated with that covenant. For example, we affix our "signature" of agreement to the new and everlasting covenant by the ordinance of baptism. Each covenant associated with the new and everlasting covenant is also "*a* new and *an* everlasting covenant"[163] because all such covenants are revealed anew to each recipient, and because they are everlasting in nature.

---

159 Smith, *History of the Church*, 5:298.
160 D&C 42:67.
161 D&C 22; 132:6–7.
162 D&C 39:11; 45:9; 66:2; 133:57.
163 *Encyclopedia of Mormonism*, 1008; D&C 22; 132:4.

Enos was one who entered into the new and everlasting covenant and thereafter exemplified the Covenant's two purposes. First, Enos obtained the assurance of his personal salvation; then he sought to bring his family into the Covenant; and finally he sought to bring other people into the Covenant.[164] Thereafter, the Lord told him that his response to the Covenant was both a proper and a universal response shared by other faithful souls: "And the Lord said unto me: Thy fathers have also required of me this thing; and it shall be done unto them according to their faith; for their faith was like unto thine."[165] Clearly, we see Zion in his life: the attributes of making saving covenants, being purified and sanctified by those covenants, and inviting other people to also make the covenants.

Centuries earlier, Abraham's response to the Covenant was similar. He also wanted to move beyond personal salvation and desired to administer the Covenant to other people so as to invite them into the lifestyle of Zion. For that reason, he sought for his "appointment unto the Priesthood." After listing a number of supernal blessings that the priesthood had to offer, Abraham rejoiced in his desire to possess this authority so that he could "administer the same."[166] That is, he wanted to administer the Covenant and the priesthood to other people so that they, too, could gain their salvation. Throughout the scriptures, we read of other righteous individuals who followed the twofold purpose of the Covenant. They sought to enter it for their personal redemption, and, once they had experienced redemption, they sought to introduce others to the Covenant for their redemption. Their hearts were changed, and they were transformed from naturally selfish people into selfless saviors on Mount Zion.

The Structure of the Covenant

The Father instituted the covenant of mercy to rescue and exalt his children. Remember, the agent of salvation is Jesus Christ; the vehicle of salvation is the Atonement, which establishes the foundation of the covenant of mercy. Upon that foundation, the new and everlasting covenant rises and forms the framework of our new life in Christ. Helaman explains, "And now, my sons, remember, remember that it is upon the rock of our Redeemer, who is Christ, the Son of God, that ye must build your foundation; that when the devil shall send forth his mighty winds, yea, his shafts in the whirlwind, yea, when all his hail and his mighty storm shall beat upon you, it shall have no power over you to drag you down to the gulf of misery and endless wo, because of the rock upon which ye are built, which is a sure foundation, a foundation whereon if men build they cannot fall."[167]

Our new life is like a temple. As that new structure rises, other covenants are added. If we were to attempt to outline the new and everlasting covenant, it might look like this:

---

164   Enos 1:4–17.
165   Enos 1:18.
166   Abraham 1:2–4.
167   Helaman 5:12.

New and Everlasting Covenant
1. Covenant of baptism
2. Oath and covenant of the priesthood
   a. Ordination (men)
   b. Temple covenants (men and women)
   c. Eternal marriage covenant (men and women)

Of profound importance is the fact that we make the new and everlasting covenant at the time of baptism with the Father, the Son, and the Holy Ghost. All three members of the Godhead effectively "affix" their names to the agreement with a covenant to save and exalt us. This is the purpose of the new and everlasting covenant. Each member of the Godhead now takes a part in our advancement and transformation, although "we receive all of the blessings of this covenant through the Son, who is Everlasting."[168] Forming a bookend to the baptismal covenant is the other covenant to which the Father, the Son, and the Holy Ghost "affix" their names: the covenant of eternal marriage. Now the new and everlasting covenant is complete. Clearly, we become Zion people by means of the Covenant—a combination of our best efforts and the best efforts of the Father, the Son, and the Holy Ghost.

The New and Everlasting Covenant As an Agreement

Imagine the Covenant as a traditional contract. By taking some liberties, let us take what we have learned about the Covenant and cast it in the form of an agreement. Much of what we note in this contract has been said before, but it may be helpful to view it in this context.

1. Introduction

The purposes of the new and everlasting covenant are to save us from the effects of the Fall and from the consequences of our sins; to turn our weaknesses into strengths; to place us beyond all our enemies and every adversity; to transform us from natural men, who are carnal, sensual, and devilish, to Saints, who are justified to receive blessings by obedience to God's laws; to make our hearts pure; to sanctify, exalt, and bless us with the fulness of God's glory;[169] and to make us all that the Father is and give us all that he has.

The Father sets the terms of the Covenant; the Son presides over, administers, and makes the Covenant operational; the Holy Ghost instructs us regarding the Covenant, makes and judges us worthy of the Covenant's blessings, and ratifies and seals the terms of the Covenant so that these blessings endure eternally. Because God's "house is a house of order . . . and not a house of confusion,"[170] he stipulates

---

168 Riddle, "The New and Everlasting Covenant," 228.
169 D&C 132:6.
170 D&C 132:8.

that "all covenants, contracts, bonds, obligations, oaths, vows, performances, connections, associations, or expectations," in the new and everlasting covenant must be "entered into and sealed by the Holy Spirit of promise [the Holy Ghost]." This sealing is done by means of the priesthood keys residing in the Lord's anointed servant, the President of the Church, who holds the exclusive right to bind in heaven what is done on earth. Otherwise, without the authority of the priesthood and the subsequent ratification of the Holy Ghost, no covenant is binding "after the resurrection from the dead; for all contracts that are not made unto this end have an end when men are dead."[171]

Through delegation of those priesthood keys, we enter the Covenant by baptism at the hands of one of Jesus Christ's servants. Because this servant holds the priesthood, he is authorized to perform the ordinance as if he were Jesus Christ: "whether by mine own voice or by the voice of my servants, it is the same."[172] This servant also has the authority to effectively "affix" the names of the three members of the Godhead—the Father, the Son, and the Holy Ghost—to this agreement: "Having been commissioned of Jesus Christ, I baptize you in the name of the Father, and of the Son, and of the Holy Ghost. Amen."[173] Our "signature," signifying our agreeing to the terms of the Covenant, is symbolized by our receiving the associated ordinance (baptism). Receiving any covenant's associated ordinance to signify our agreement becomes the pattern for our making all other saving covenants within the new and everlasting covenant. Fulfilling the terms of any covenant justifies us for that covenant's attendant blessings.

The new and everlasting covenant is the Father's response to the demands of justice. To rescue and protect us from the consequences of broken celestial laws, and to allow us to progress, regain our bodies, and be preserved by obedience to celestial law, the Father provides the covenant of mercy. Mercy calls for a Savior to atone for us. The new and everlasting covenant is the agreement we make with the Father to access the blessings of the Atonement. The new and everlasting covenant consists of two major covenants: the covenant of baptism, and the oath and covenant of the priesthood. The priesthood covenant, which is initially made by worthy men at the time of ordination, expands to eventually include both men and women. These additional priesthood covenants are those taken by worthy men and women in the temple, culminating with the covenant of eternal marriage.

2. The Covenant of Justice

The covenant of justice provides that the Father will reveal to us the immutable laws that govern him and all celestial beings. These laws comprise the pattern of his lifestyle, which set of laws allows him to be both perfect and perfectly *just*. By obeying these same laws we adopt his lifestyle and can become like him.

---

171 D&C 132:7.
172 D&C 1:38.
173 D&C 20:73.

The Father has decreed an *umbrella law* to govern all other laws. This law provides that all laws of God must contain two things: immutable blessings and immutable punishments. By accepting the covenant of justice, we agree that God: (1) is the supreme lawgiver; (2) his laws are just; and (3) we will accept the consequences of obedience or disobedience to his laws.

The covenant of justice functions on the principle of agency. By choice we demonstrate our obedience, which is likewise demonstrated by our willingness to sacrifice in order to obey. It is by choice, therefore, that we become both just and justified for blessings or cursings.

Blessings for Obedience

The covenant of justice is harsh when disobeyed but glorious when obeyed. By obedience to any law of God, we are justified to receive the blessing associated with that law. Moreover, we are preserved, perfected, and sanctified by obedience to God's law.[174] This is the covenant by which men and women are justified to "gain an inheritance in the Kingdom of God."[175]

3. The Covenant of Mercy

The covenant of mercy, or the new and everlasting covenant, was established by the Father in response to the demands made by the covenant of justice. The covenant of mercy is the law of God that has the power to "appease the demands of justice,"[176] if obeyed. The primary stipulations associated with the covenant of mercy are these: (1) We agree to accept Jesus Christ and his Atonement by exercising faith in Jesus Christ; (2) We agree to repent and change our lives; (3) We agree to enter into the new and everlasting covenant through baptism and thereafter to enter likewise into all other saving covenants; (4) We agree to receive the Holy Ghost and yield to his efforts to purify us, sanctify us, and to make us fit in every way for celestial glory.

Blessings for Obedience

Because we desire deliverance from the world and rescue from the effects of our sinful choices, we seek mercy. The only source of that mercy is Jesus Christ. Like all laws of God, the covenant of mercy contains both a blessing and a punishment. If we obey the laws associated with this covenant, we receive forgiveness of sins, reconciliation to God, and inheritance in his kingdom, which includes all that he has and is. If we disobey the law associated with this covenant, we receive damnation, and we alone must pay the price of our sins.[177]

The covenant of mercy allows us to embrace the covenant of justice without being destroyed by the laws of God that we break. Therefore, the covenant of mercy

---

174   D&C 88:34–35.
175   McConkie, *Mormon Doctrine*, 117.
176   Alma 42:15.
177   D&C 19:15–20.

provides a Savior to atone for us. The Atonement of Jesus Christ provides us a sure foundation upon which we can build a new life that will become worthy of God's presence and inheritance in his kingdom.

Upon our accepting the Atonement and entering into the new and everlasting covenant by baptism, the Savior meets the demands of justice for every sin that we have committed or will commit. He provides us the supernal gift of the Holy Ghost to purify, sanctify, and justify us, and to transform us into perfect beings like our Father. The Savior provides us his grace to make up for what our best effort will not cover. Additionally, he reconciles us to God so that nothing stands between us and the Father and so that we can one day appear before God without guilt, shame, spot, or blemish.

The covenant of mercy, or the new and everlasting covenant, forms the defined path that leads to eternal life, places in our hands the authority of God, gives us access to God's knowledge and power, and establishes us in our eternal kingdom. To accomplish these objectives, the covenant of mercy provides us two additional primary covenants: the covenant of baptism, and the oath and covenant of the priesthood.

4. The Covenant of Baptism

To receive power to leave behind our lives in Babylon, and to "fulfill all righteousness"[178] by being born again into a new life, we agree to exercise faith in Jesus Christ, repent of our sins, and follow the Savior's example of entering into the new and everlasting covenant by means of the ordinance of baptism by immersion.[179]

By baptism, we signify our agreement to become an adopted son or daughter of Jesus Christ, spiritually begotten[180] of him to become part of his family. We agree to take upon ourselves the name of Jesus Christ, our new spiritual father. We agree to always remember him and to keep his commandments, including every word that proceeds from the mouth of God.[181] We agree to become active, sustaining members of Christ's family, the earthly name of which is The Church of Jesus Christ of Latter-day Saints. This family, or Church, is God's kingdom on earth. Furthermore, we agree to stand as witnesses of God, to bear one another's burdens, to mourn with those who mourn, to comfort those who stand in need of comfort, to manifest a determination to serve God to the end, and to receive the Holy Ghost to facilitate the process by which we are purified of our sins. We agree to submit to the Holy Ghost's purifying and sanctifying efforts to transform us into new creatures.[182] We agree to renew our baptismal covenant by making the covenant associated with the sacrament.

---

178 Matthew 3:15.
179 Articles of Faith 1:4.
180 Mosiah 5:7.
181 D&C 20:77; 84:44.
182 Mosiah 5:7; 18:7–10; 27:24–26.

Section 2   The New and Everlasting Covenant—The First Pillar of Zion

Blessings for Obedience

Baptism provides us an initial and immediate remission of our sins.[183] We are *born again*[184] into the family of Jesus Christ. We entered physical life by the breaking of the birth water, the entrance of our spirits into our bodies, and by the issue of blood; in baptism we are born again by the water (baptism), of the spirit (Holy Ghost), and of the blood (the Atonement of Jesus Christ).[185] We become members of Jesus Christ's family (The Church of Jesus Christ of Latter-day Saints), and receive him as our adopted spiritual father.[186]

Thereafter, by a holy ordinance (confirmation), our membership in our new family is *confirmed*, or made sure.[187] As part of the confirmation ordinance, we are commanded to receive the Holy Ghost. This is the Spirit that enters our new "selves" and makes us "alive in Christ."[188] As long as we remain worthy, the Holy Ghost will be our guide, comforter, companion, testator, revelator, justifier, purifier, and sanctifier. The Holy Ghost will teach us the truth of all things[189] and give us power to keep the terms of the Covenant and every covenant within the Covenant. He will burn out of us, as if by fire, all iniquity, carnality, sensuality, and every evil thing, so that we might become perfectly fit for eternal life.[190] The Holy Ghost will make of us a new being capable of standing spotless before God in the Day of Judgment.[191]

By baptism, we enter in at the gate, where Jesus is the gatekeeper,[192] which gate opens onto the path called *strait and narrow*.[193] This path leads to the celestial kingdom. If we endure in faithfulness in the new and everlasting covenant, we will experience the highest manifestation of salvation:[194] eternal life and exaltation.[195] By continuing obedience to terms of the covenant of baptism, we will become the "redeemed of God, . . . numbered with those of the first [celestial] resurrection" and "have eternal life."[196]

4a) Agreement to Renew and Abide in the Covenant of Baptism

To "retain a remission of sins,"[197] we agree to "remember, and always retain in remembrance, the greatness of God."[198] We agree to always remember Jesus Christ,

---

183   D&C 13.
184   John 3:3, 7.
185   Moses 6:59–60.
186   Mosiah 5:7.
187   Bible Dictionary, "Confirmation," 649.
188   2 Nephi 25:25.
189   Moroni 10:5.
190   3 Nephi 27:24–26.
191   3 Nephi 27:20.
192   2 Nephi 9:41.
193   McConkie, Conference Report, Oct. 1955, 12; 2 Nephi 31:18.
194   2 Nephi 9:23–24; 31:13–21.
195   2 Nephi 31:20.
196   Mosiah 18:9.
197   Mosiah 4:12; JST, Matthew 26:22–25; JST, Mark 14:20–25; JST, Luke 22:17–20.
198   Mosiah 4:12.

specifically his sacrificed body and the blood he gave to redeem us.[199] The sacrament is the ordinance that signifies this remembrance.

By this ordinance, we renew our covenant of baptism, which is at the same time a renewal of the new and everlasting covenant. To that end, we agree to worthily and willingly partake of "the emblems of the flesh and blood of Christ"[200] as the priests administer them. We agree to (1) again take upon us the name of Christ; (2) always remember Jesus, his broken body, sacrificed blood, teachings, example, and love for us; and (3) renew and keep the agreements that we made at baptism.

To retain a remission of our sins, we agree to walk in all humility, remembering our own nothingness and the Lord's goodness and long-suffering toward us; we agree to call upon the name of the Lord daily and to stand steadfastly "in the faith of that which has been wrought for us by the Atonement of Jesus Christ."[201]

Blessings for Obedience

The sacrament is the ordinance that renews the terms of the baptismal covenant, which is the entrance covenant into the new and everlasting covenant. Moreover, the sacrament is the ordinance that assures us of retaining the gift of the Holy Ghost. By obedience to the sacramental covenant, we qualify to always have the Lord's Spirit—the Holy Ghost—to be with us. Therefore, the presence of the Holy Ghost in our lives is given to us as a special sign that we are yet retaining a remission of sins by the merits and grace of Jesus Christ.[202] This allows us to progress in the Covenant toward perfection and receive blessings without having yet achieved perfection. In the sacramental covenant, the Lord blesses us that in due course we shall inherit eternal life.[203]

We receive the blessing of receiving the Lord's gifts. Symbolically, we come to the sacramental table to exchange gifts: we offer the Lord our hearts, and he offers us emblems, or tokens, that represent the sacrifice that he made for us. By worthily partaking of the sacrament, the Lord blesses us with the fruits[204] and gifts of the Spirit.[205]

4b) Agreement to Live the Law of the Sabbath Day

As a special sign that we have entered into the new and everlasting covenant by baptism, we agree to "remember the Sabbath day, to keep it holy."[206] This law has always been associated with covenant people. By keeping this law, we indicate that we are separate, distinct, and known to the world as covenant people.[207] By living this law, we keep ourselves more unspotted from the world.[208]

---

199 D&C 20:40, 77, 79.
200 D&C 20:40.
201 Mosiah 4:11.
202 2 Nephi 31:19; Moroni 6:4; D&C 3:20.
203 John 6:5–4; McConkie, *Mormon Doctrine*, 660.
204 Galatians 5:22.
205 D&C 46.
206 Exodus 20:8–11.
207 Nehemiah 13:15–22; Isaiah 56:1–8; Jeremiah 17:19–27; Ezekiel 46:1–7.
208 D&C 59:9.

We agree to acknowledge that the Sabbath day is the Lord's day,[209] which he has hallowed.[210] The law of the Sabbath day requires that we labor six days for our temporal sustenance; then, on the Sabbath day, we rest from that work and completely devote ourselves to the Lord's work and to worshipping Him. Therefore, we agree to consecrate the Sabbath day to the Lord and use that day to chart a course leading to eternal life.[211]

Because we have been commanded to "thank the Lord thy God in all things," and to "offer a sacrifice unto the Lord thy God in righteousness, even that of a broken heart and a contrite spirit,"[212] we agree to go to the house of prayer on the Sabbath day and there offer up our sacraments, meaning our personal promises to forsake our sins and failings, with the faith that if we do so, the Lord will forgive and bless us.[213] We agree to pay, on the Sabbath day, our personal and spiritual devotions and oblations unto the Lord—that is, our worship, thanks, and temporal and spiritual offerings. An oblation is an offering. "The Hebrew word . . . is to come near. The person bringing the offering does so in order to come closer to God. . . . It is in sacrament meeting as we contemplate the sacramental altar that our offering of a broken heart and a contrite spirit brings us nearer to the altar of sacrifice and reminds us of our complete dependence upon the Atonement of the Savior."[214]

On the Sabbath day, we confess "our sins unto [our] brethren, and before the Lord."[215] Partaking of the sacrament and confessing to the bishop, when necessary, qualify as two ways to fulfill this stipulation. The Sabbath day is a day to fast and bear witness of the Lord.[216] On this day, we agree to rest, that is, to enter into the Lord's rest, meaning his glory,[217] whereby we might commune with him.

Blessings for Obedience

For keeping the Sabbath day holy, the Lord will bless and prosper us beyond our comprehension.[218] He will establish and preserve our kingdom forever.[219] He will send us rain in due season. He will help us overcome our enemies, which include our weaknesses and adversities. He will bless us with peace, multiply us, and establish the Covenant with us and our succeeding generations.[220] He promises: "I will walk among you; and will be your God, and ye will be my people."[221] By obedience to the law of the Sabbath day, the Lord swears to the world that we are his chosen people and that we have entered into the everlasting Covenant.[222]

---

209 D&C 59:12.
210 Exodus 20:8–11.
211 McConkie, *A New Witness for the Articles of Faith*, 301.
212 D&C 59:8.
213 McConkie, *A New Witness for the Articles of Faith*, 301–2.
214 Cannon, "Oblation," *Mormon Times*, Feb. 5, 2009.
215 D&C 59:12.
216 D&C 59:7–13.
217 D&C 84:24.
218 McConkie, *A New Witness for the Articles of Faith*, 301.
219 Jeremiah 17:20–27.
220 Leviticus 26:2–9.
221 Isaiah 58:13–14.
222 Nehemiah 13:15–22; Isaiah 56:1–8; Jeremiah 17:19–17; Ezekiel 31:12–17.

Inasmuch as we keep the law of the Sabbath day, the earth will yield up its bounty to us: "The fulness of the earth is yours, the beasts of the field and the fowls of the air, and that which climbeth upon the trees and walketh upon the earth; yea, and the herb, and the good things which come of the earth, whether for food or for raiment, or for houses, or for barns, or for orchards, or for gardens, or for vineyards; yea, all things which come of the earth, in the season thereof, are made for the benefit and the use of man, both to please the eye and to gladden the heart; yea, for food and for raiment, for taste and for smell, to strengthen the body and to enliven the soul."[223]

As we partake of the sacrament on the Sabbath day, the Lord will count our sacrifice of a broken heart and a contrite spirit as though we had placed all things on the altar. He will forgive us of our sins, and he will help us face and overcome our weaknesses.[224] Ultimately, he will bless us to enter into his rest.[225]

5. Agreement to Receive the Covenant of the Priesthood

When we have experienced personal redemption, we (a man or a woman) agree to become saviors on Mount Zion[226] and help save both the living and the dead. To do this redemptive work, we agree to receive the blessings of the priesthood "for your sake, and not for your sake only, but for the sake of the whole world."[227]

Only worthy men receive ordination to the priesthood. When men are ordained to the Melchizedek Priesthood, they receive it by covenant and with the Father's oath: his guarantee, upon the condition of worthiness, of exaltation and the inheriting of his kingdom.[228] Men agree to magnify their calling, and the first way is through ordination, which carries with it the charge to serve others and accept and diligently fulfill other assignments and callings in the Church. The second and third ways involve both men and women.[229] These ways are receiving the temple initiatory ordinances and the priesthood endowment, and then receiving celestial marriage and thereby entering into the patriarchal order of the priesthood.

5a) Worthy Men Agree to Be Ordained

Men agree to make themselves worthy to receive both the Aaronic and Melchizedek priesthoods and thereby be called the sons of Aaron and of Moses.[230] When

---

223 D&C 59:16–19.
224 McConkie, *A New Witness for the Articles of Faith*, 301–2.
225 D&C 84:24.
226 Obadiah 1:21.
227 D&C 84:48.
228 D&C 84:37–38.
229 "Now, *as far as the Church of Christ is concerned*, this oath and covenant is made first in baptism, when the Holy Ghost is given, and more especially when the Priesthood is conferred. It is, secondly, repeated by partaking of the Sacrament, and by entering into special covenants in holy places [the temple]." (Editor's Table, "The Bondage of Sin," *Improvement Era*, Feb. 1923; emphasis added.) Also: "This covenant, made when the priesthood is received, is renewed when the recipient enters the order of eternal marriage." (McConkie, *A New Witness for the Articles of Faith*, 313.)
230 D&C 84:34.

men are ordained to the Melchizedek Priesthood, Jesus Christ will place upon them his name,[231] allowing those men to minister as if they were Jesus Christ.

Ordained men agree to remember that "the rights of the priesthood are inseparably connected with the powers of heaven, and that the powers of heaven cannot be controlled nor handled only upon the principles of righteousness." Therefore, they agree not to set their hearts upon the things of this world; neither will they undertake to cover their sins, to gratify their pride, their vain ambition, nor to exercise control or dominion or compulsion upon the souls of the children of men, in any degree of unrighteousness. Rather, as the Lord's authorized servants and thus representing him, ordained men agree to exercise gentle persuasion, long-suffering, gentleness, meekness, love unfeigned, kindness, and pure knowledge, which greatly enlarges the soul without hypocrisy or guile. When ordained men need to occasionally reprove with sharpness, they agree to do so only when moved upon by the Holy Ghost and then show forth afterward an increase of love toward him whom they have reproved. Ordained men agree to extend charity toward all people, to their own families, and to the household of faith, who are the members of the Church, the family of Jesus Christ.

They agree to let virtue garnish their thoughts unceasingly.[232]

Blessings for Obedience

Worthy ordained men become "priest[s] of the Most High . . . after the order of Melchizedek."[233] They receive the right, when called upon, to preside in the offices of the Aaronic and the Melchizedek priesthoods. They are blessed to have Jesus Christ place upon them his own name[234] and his authority, which is the right to act in his name under the direction of priesthood leaders who hold the keys to this authority. They receive the "power of God to act in all things for the benefit of mankind, both in and out of the world."[235]

Holding the Aaronic Priesthood, ordained men have the authority to administer in outward ordinances[236] such as baptism and the sacrament. They are also authorized to teach, expound, exhort, and watch over the Church always—being with and strengthening members, seeing that there is no iniquity or hardness with each other, no lying, backbiting, or evil-speaking; to see that the Church meets together often and that the members attend to their duties; to assist the higher priesthood and take the lead when no elder is present.[237] And they are entitled to the ministering of angels.[238]

Holding the Melchizedek Priesthood, ordained men are now empowered to resume their premortal work, which Catherine Thomas said was the work of

---

231 Abraham 1:18.
232 Adapted from D&C 121:35–37, 41–45.
233 D&C 76:57–58.
234 Abraham 1:18.
235 *Encyclopedia of Mormonism*, 1134.
236 D&C 107:13–14.
237 D&C 20:46–56.
238 D&C 84:26.

redemption,[239] and thereafter to continue on with that work in eternity, being kings and priests unto God forever.[240] They have the right of presidency, should they be called upon, because this higher priesthood has authority to officiate in all the offices in the Church. Being Melchizedek Priesthood holders, they have authority to administer the "spiritual blessings of the church."[241] This high priesthood has the power to administer "endless lives to the sons and daughters of Adam."[242]

Ordained men have the authority to confirm the children of God members of the Church of Jesus Christ and to confer upon them the gift of the Holy Ghost. Additionally, they have the authority, under the direction of priesthood leaders called to leadership positions (presidencies), to take the lead in meetings of the Church and to ordain other worthy men to offices in the priesthood.[243]

By giving diligence to their ordination, their confidence will wax strong in God's presence; and the "doctrine of the priesthood shall distill upon" their souls like the dews from heaven. "The Holy Ghost shall be [their] constant companion, and [their] scepter an unchanging scepter of righteousness and truth." Their celestial dominion shall be everlasting, "and without compulsory means it shall flow unto [them] forever and ever."[244]

Ordained men are empowered to become as the Father and the Son are—gods, in their own right. They can achieve this exalted status upon the same principle that the Father and the Son gained their exaltation: by receiving the same oath and keeping this same covenant.

5b) Ordained Men Agree to Magnify Their Calling

Melchizedek Priesthood holders agree to magnify their calling in the kingdom of God by taking their responsibilities seriously, making those responsibilities honorable in the eyes of God's children and glorious to God.[245] They agree to function faithfully under the guidance of priesthood leadership and the instruction of the Holy Ghost.[246]

Because the primary *calling* is the call to eternal life, they agree to become like God. They agree to accomplish this by going to the temple to be cleansed, purified, set apart, and prepared for that purpose so that they might be initiated into the order of the gods. They continue by being endowed with keys to God's knowledge and power. Then they agree to receive the crowning event that enables them to become like God: entering into eternal marriage. These steps facilitate the fulfillment of their calling, and they magnify that calling by obedience and diligence.

---

239 Thomas, "Alma the Younger, Part 1," n.p.
240 D&C 76:56–57; 138:57.
241 D&C 107:8, 10.
242 Smith, *Teachings of the Prophet Joseph Smith*, 322.
243 D&C 20:39–45.
244 D&C 121:45–46.
245 *Encyclopedia of Mormonism*, 850.
246 Riddle, "The New and Everlasting Covenant," 232.

Blessings for Obedience

If ordained men magnify their *calling* faithfully, they will be given progressively greater authority and power, and they will shoulder increasing responsibility in their stewardships, which may or may not by manifested in Church positions.[247]

Because the *calling* of an ordained Melchizedek Priesthood holder is to be "*called* into the fellowship of Jesus Christ,"[248] and because such men were "*called* and prepared from the foundation of the world according to the foreknowledge of God, on account of their exceeding faith and good works,"[249] if they continue faithful they receive the blessing on earth to be *called* and elected (selected) for eternal life. For that purpose, they are blessed to go to the holy temple and receive sanctifying ordinances. These include being cleansed, purified, set apart, prepared, and initiated into the order of the gods. Additionally, they are endowed with keys to the knowledge and power of God,[250] and they are established in their eternal kingdoms by entering into the highest order of the priesthood—the patriarchal order—which is the new and everlasting covenant of marriage.[251]

5c) Ordained Men Agree to Continued Faithfulness

Ordained men agree to "keep the commandments of God, to live by every word that proceedeth forth from the mouth of Deity, and to walk in paths of righteousness and virtue."[252]

Blessings for Obedience

Worthy ordained men (and worthy women) make up "the church and kingdom, and the elect of God,"[253] having premortally received the "election of grace."[254] This means that in the premortal realm they qualified to be selected in this life to receive the new and everlasting covenant for their own salvation and that they were selected to administer the Covenant to others so that they, too, could be saved.[255] To that end, they become "the seed of Abraham,"[256] and are thus entitled to all the blessings of Abraham, Isaac, and Jacob. These blessings include the right for their posterity to become "lawful heirs" to the fulness of priesthood and gospel blessings "according to the flesh."[257]

The Holy Ghost will purify and sanctify worthy ordained men unto the renewing of their bodies,[258] thus enlivening and strengthening them so that they might

---

247 Riddle, "The New and Everlasting Covenant," 232; Matthew 25:14–30.
248 1 Corinthians 1:9, 26–27; emphasis added; Hebrews 3:1.
249 Alma 13:3–5; emphasis added.
250 D&C 95:8.
251 D&C 131:1–4.
252 McConkie, *Mormon Doctrine*, 480.
253 D&C 84:34.
254 D&C 84:98–102; Romans 11:1–5.
255 Romans 9:11; 11:5, 7, 28.
256 D&C 84:34.
257 D&C 86:8–11; 113:6.
258 D&C 84:33.

administer the Covenant to other people.[259] Furthermore, they are renewed by being married for eternity and by means of the posterity born to them in the Covenant. Worthy ordained men will enter into the Lord's *rest*, which is "the fulness of his glory."[260] They will receive the Father's kingdom, and, thus, all that he has and is shall be theirs.[261]

During their sojourn on this earth, ordained men are entitled to revelation for their personal lives and for their stewardships.[262] They are entitled "to have the privilege of receiving the mysteries of the kingdom of heaven, to have the heavens opened unto them, to commune with the general assembly and Church of the Firstborn, and to enjoy the communion and presence of God the Father, and Jesus, the mediator of the new covenant."[263] Moreover, they are entitled to the ministering of angels for guidance, protection, and instruction.[264]

6. Abide in the Covenant to the End

Now that we have made the covenants of baptism and the priesthood, we agree to abide in the new and everlasting covenant to the end, and to give strict diligence to making our calling and election sure. We agree to be perfect as the Father is perfect;[265] that is, we agree to abide in the Covenant with as much diligence as does the Father, "even unto death, that you may be found worthy."[266] We agree to fiercely pursue the "strait and narrow path" "with unshaken faith in [Christ], relying wholly upon the merits of him who is mighty to save." We agree to "press forward with a steadfastness in Christ, having a perfect brightness of hope, and a love of God and of all men." The Father has decreed that "this is the way; and there is none other way nor name given under heaven whereby man can be saved in the kingdom of God." Furthermore, "this is the doctrine of Christ, and the only and true doctrine of the Father, and of the Son, and of the Holy Ghost, which is one God, without end."[267]

Blessings for Enduring to the End

If we keep all the terms of the new and everlasting covenant, including all of the Lord's commandments, and if we receive and obey all the ordinances of the house of the Lord, we will receive a "fulness of the priesthood" and become heirs of God and joint heirs with Jesus Christ.[268] "Those holding the fulness of the Melchizedek Priesthood are kings and priests [women are queens and priestesses] of the Most

---

259 *Encyclopedia of Mormonism*, 1019.
260 D&C 84:24.
261 D&C 84:35–38.
262 D&C 84:44.
263 D&C 107:19.
264 D&C 84:42.
265 Matthew 5:48.
266 D&C 98:14.
267 2 Nephi 31:17–21.
268 Smith, *Teachings of the Prophet Joseph Smith*, 308–9.

High God, holding the keys of power and blessing."[269] If we will do this, "feasting upon the word of Christ, and endure to the end, behold, thus saith the Father: Ye shall have eternal life."[270]

The Father's Guarantee

If we will abide in the new and everlasting covenant, the Father promises by his own name, putting his own Godhood on the line,[271] that, upon our faithfulness, he will fulfill every promise that he has made herein: "I, the Lord, am bound when ye do what I say; but when ye do not what I say, ye have no promise."[272] Therefore, he unequivocally promises that if we do our part, we shall have eternal life.[273]

Effective Signatures

We agree to the terms of the new and everlasting covenant by receiving the ordinance of baptism. The Father, the Son, and the Holy Ghost effectively affix their names to the Covenant when the officiating priesthood holder invokes their names in the baptismal ordinance.[274]

The foregoing is an attempt to help the reader understand the new and everlasting covenant as an agreement. Without the Atonement of Jesus Christ, the Covenant would be meaningless; but, built upon that sure foundation, the Covenant has the power to transform, save, and exalt God's children.

We must keep in mind that learning of the Covenant and living it are processes. Because we have listed the elements of the Covenant in superlative terms that define the ideal, we might become tempted to become discouraged because of our present location on the path. But we must remember that the Lord's mercy includes his grace. Therefore, our forward movement is more important than whether or not we have arrived yet. Blessings come by trying and improving; we are rewarded through grace as if we had achieved the ideal—and we likewise receive grace to help us in our efforts to improve along the way. "For behold, thus saith the Lord God: I will give unto the children of men line upon line, precept upon precept, here a little and there a little; and blessed are those who hearken unto my precepts, and lend an ear unto my counsel, for they shall learn wisdom; for unto him that receiveth I will give more."[275] Hence, regardless of our present situation, Zion is ever within our grasp.

---

269 Smith, *Teachings of the Prophet Joseph Smith*, 322.
270 2 Nephi 31:20.
271 McConkie, *A New Witness for the Articles of Faith*, 317.
272 D&C 82:10.
273 2 Nephi 31:20.
274 Articles of Faith 1:5.
275 2 Nephi 28:30.

Section 3
Abide in the Covenant

Of unparalleled significance is the fact that the Father created the new and everlasting covenant.[276] He established it for the salvation of his children, and to that end he set the unalterable terms that result in the absolute promise of exaltation: "And as pertaining to the new and everlasting covenant, it was instituted for the fulness of my glory; and he that receiveth a fulness thereof must and shall abide the law."[277] No one having received the Covenant can thereafter deny or reject it without experiencing serious and eternal consequences: "I reveal unto you a new and an everlasting covenant; and if ye abide not that covenant, then are ye damned; for no one can reject this covenant and be permitted to enter into my glory."[278] Our ability to become Zion people and our eternal future hinge upon our diligence in keeping the terms of the new and everlasting covenant: "I have decreed in my heart, saith the Lord, that I will prove you in all things, whether you will abide in my covenant, even unto death, that you may be found worthy. For if ye will not abide in my covenant ye are not worthy of me."[279]

An additional thought-provoking verity is found in the oath and covenant of the priesthood: if we will abide ("remain in a place, and continue to be sure or firm"[280]) in the Covenant, the Father himself will teach us regarding it.[281] This astonishing idea speaks to the importance that the Father places on the new and everlasting covenant. Truly, it is by this Covenant that he accomplishes this work that glorifies him.[282]

The deeper we dig into the doctrine of the Covenant, the more we discover a loving relationship. A caring Father is offering us all that he has and is. To that end, he reveals the laws by which he lives, which are the commandments that he gives us, and he offers us the same eternal covenants of progression and exaltation that made him who he is. He knows that the Covenant will help us grow from dependence to independence. For

---

276 3 Nephi 16:5; 20:12, 25, 27, 29, 46; 21:4, 7; 29:1; Mormon 5:14; 9:47; Ether 4:15; Moroni 10:33; D&C 84:40.
277 D&C 132:6.
278 D&C 132:4; see also verse 6.
279 D&C 98:14–15.
280 *American Heritage Dictionary*, s.v. "abide."
281 D&C 84:48.
282 Moses 1:39.

all these reasons, he invites us into a covenantal relationship, whereby we, together with him, share his order of life and his pattern of celestial living. This is Zion!

Most certainly, Heavenly Father fully dedicates himself to offering us the Covenant, teaching us its intricacies, and walking with us step by step toward the Covenant's stated purpose: immortality and eternal life.[283] At each significant event along the way, "to fulfill all righteousness,"[284] we meet with him, often at an altar, of our own free will, to exchange vows and gifts. We promise to give our hearts, and he promises to give us tokens and emblems, *treasures* that help us to remember his gift of a Savior and to retain in our remembrance the infinite price that was paid by the Father and the Son to make the Covenant possible. Moreover, by the Covenant we become *his* "peculiar treasures"[285] by treasuring up the words of eternal life[286] for the everlasting salvation of our souls in the kingdom of God.[287] By the Covenant, he *calls* us out of the world and separates us for a holy purpose, so that one day he might elect (select) us for the highest manifestation of salvation called eternal life.

Clearly, the Covenant is all about *relationship*. Broadly, the relationship is called *Zion*, a celestial condition and an order of pure-hearted individuals who live in eternal marriages and families. The members of such families are pure, happy, and unselfish. They increase in number and in joy forever. To make these relationships sure and to confirm, or "make sure," the terms of the Covenant, three distinct offerings must be made:

1. The Father offers to share with us the supernal blessings of the Covenant.
2. The Son offers to cover the infinite expenses of the Covenant that we cannot meet.
3. We offer our hearts.

Yielding our hearts to God allows us to be assimilated into the celestial order. We do this by living the celestial laws of Zion in a telestial world, adopting the Father's work of redemption as our own, and becoming experts at serving and saving his children. As covenant people, our responsibility is to draw the Father's children into a holy circle of the oneness indicative of Zion: a circle that is safe, secure, peaceful, cooperative, merciful, charitable, and unified.

The Leavening Power of the Doctrine of the Covenant

After yet another run-in with the Pharisees, Jesus and the disciples entered into a boat to depart to the other side of the Sea of Galilee. This incident had been preceded by the Savior's feeding of four thousand men and their wives and families—the second time he had miraculously fed thousands with few resources. As the disciples were sailing to the other side, they discovered that they had taken with them only a single loaf of bread, hardly enough to feed thirteen men. Jesus seized this teaching opportunity by connecting an ingredient of the

---

283 Moses 1:39.
284 Matthew 3:15.
285 Exodus 19:5; Psalms 135:4.
286 D&C 6:20; 84:5.
287 D&C 11:3; 12:3; 14:3.

bread with the doctrine of the Pharisees, whom they had just left: "And he charged them, saying, Take heed, beware of the leaven of the Pharisees, and of the leaven of Herod." Of course, leaven is yeast, the ingredient that expands quickly throughout the bread dough, making it rise. The connection of leaven to the Pharisees' doctrine escaped the disciples, "and they reasoned among themselves, saying, It is because we have no bread."

We can hear some frustration in Jesus' reply to their inability to see past their hunger: "Why reason ye, because ye have no bread? perceive ye not yet, neither understand? have ye your heart yet hardened? Having eyes, see ye not? and having ears, hear ye not? and do ye not remember?"

Then came the lesson.

"When I brake the five loaves among five thousand, how many baskets full of fragments took ye up? They say unto him, Twelve. And when the seven among four thousand, how many baskets full of fragments took ye up? And they said, Seven. And he said unto them, How is it that ye do not understand?"[288]

The lesson might escape us, too, if it were not for Matthew's account of the incident: "How is it that ye do not understand that I spake it not to you concerning bread, that ye should beware of the leaven of the Pharisees and of the Sadducees? Then understood they how that he bade them not beware of the leaven of bread, but of the doctrine of the Pharisees and of the Sadducees."[289]

Words are like leaven! Once planted in the soul, they grow. Leaven is like the good seed Alma describes; if nourished, the seed will begin to swell, then to sprout, and eventually to grow into a tree bearing delicious fruit.[290] Both leaven and the seed are small things that become great things. On the other hand, if the words of Satan are planted and remain in the soul, they will take root and grow into a briarlike tangle that becomes destructive.

Once the doctrine of the Covenant takes hold in the fertile ground of a receptive soul, the Father will come and teach us its sublime intricacies[291] and empower us to abide in its precepts. More and more, the Covenant becomes a part of us, until we are totally "leavened" by it. Given a chance to grow, the Covenant will make of us Zion people. As we become Zion people by the leavening power of the Covenant, we feel no urge to be drawn back to the great and spacious building or the filthy river or the mists of darkness, which also describe the church of the devil and Babylon. Zion simply looks and feels better than anything Babylon has to offer.

The Covenant Separates Us from Babylon, or the World

When we enter into the new and everlasting covenant by baptism, we are *born again* into a new life.[292] That life is a Zion life. Baptism symbolizes death and rebirth, or resurrection.[293] That is, we *die* as to our old life and are born into a new life with a new spiritual

---

288 Mark 8:10–21.
289 Matthew 16:11–12.
290 Alma 32:28–41.
291 D&C 84:48.
292 Mosiah 27:25; Alma 7:14; Moses 6:59; John 3:3–7.
293 *Encyclopedia of Mormonism*, 93.

father, Jesus Christ, and a new family, the Church of Jesus Christ.[294] We are, and must remain forever, separate and unique, the Lord's peculiar treasure[295] and his covenant people. Alma taught, "And now I say unto you, all you that are desirous to follow the voice of the good shepherd, come ye out from the wicked, and be ye separate, and touch not their unclean things; and behold, their names shall be blotted out, that the names of the wicked shall not be numbered among the names of the righteous, that the word of God may be fulfilled, which saith: The names of the wicked shall not be mingled with the names of my people."[296]

In our former, "natural man" life, we were identified with Babylon, but in our new life, we must never be identified with Babylon again. We are Zion now, separate and distinct. The kingdom of which we are now a part is "not of this world."[297] We, like Jesus, our spiritual father, must overcome the world "by valuing spiritual wealth and eternal treasure above earthly goods and attainments."[298] Whereas Babylon people are distinguished by "works of the flesh," such as "adultery, fornication, uncleanness, lasciviousness, idolatry, witchcraft, hatred, variance, emulations, wrath, strife, seditions, heresies, envyings, murders, drunkenness, revellings, and such," Zion people are distinguished by the fruits of the Spirit: "love, joy, peace, longsuffering, gentleness, goodness, faith, meekness, temperance."[299]

Zion people are commissioned to invite others out of Babylon and into Zion so that they too might partake of the Covenant and be saved. Just as the Father sent his Son into the world to offer the Covenant to the people of the world, so Jesus (beginning with his Apostles) sends us into the world to offer the Covenant.[300] We have no business allowing ourselves to be seduced or drawn back to Babylon in any degree. By doing so, we abandon our Covenant and commit treason against Zion.[301]

Zion People Are Distinguished by Observing the Sabbath Day

As mentioned, the Sabbath day is a *sign* that distinguishes and identifies us as people of the Covenant. By keeping the law of the Sabbath day, we signify among other things, that we have abandoned Babylon in favor of Zion and that we intend to remain separate and distinct from the world. We have no desire to be "spotted" or contaminated by associating with the world.[302] Moreover, we live Zion's law of consecration, in part, by consecrating this day—the Lord's day[303]—to him to do his work and no other. This is a concept completely foreign to Babylon, whose philosophy is to make profit, seek pleasure, and indulge in self-serving activities twenty-four hours a day, every day, including the

---

294 Moses 5:7.
295 Exodus 19:5; Psalms 135:4.
296 Alma 5:57.
297 John 18:36.
298 *Encyclopedia of Mormonism*, 1587.
299 Galatians 5:19–23.
300 John 17:18.
301 Smith, *Teachings of the Prophet Joseph Smith*, 348–49.
302 D&C 59:9.
303 D&C 59:12.

Sabbath day. On the Sabbath, Zion people worship their God, while Babylon people worship the idols of moneymaking ventures and pleasure.

On the Sabbath day, Zion people go to the house of God to express gratitude to him, to offer to him the sacrifice of a broken heart and a contrite spirit, to confess to him their sins, to fast and bear testimony of God, and thereby enter into his rest.

Conversely, Babylon people serve a different god on the Sabbath day. Babylon people cheer for the home team, indulge, play, shop, camp, and barbeque; they worship their boats, go rock climbing, escape into nature, watch television, go to movies, and do anything to gratify themselves. On the Sabbath day, Babylon people lounge or sleep whereas Zion people *rest*.

For the obedience of the people of Zion, the Lord blesses them with rain in due season and with protection from their enemies and from adversity; he blesses them with peace and with abundance in family and in the good things of the earth; he will grant their posterity the right to the blessings of the Covenant; he will bless them with his presence and call them his *chosen*. The earth will yield up its bounty to Zion people who live the law of the Sabbath day.

On the other hand, by mocking the Sabbath day, Babylon receives the Lord's curse and spiritual death.

Power in the Covenant

In a sweeping vision of the last days, Nephi saw us, the latter-day followers of the Lamb of God, as the objects of Satan's wrath. Our righteousness became our defense, righteousness which summoned the power of God and in turn empowered us to withstand the adversary so that we might go forth and accomplish our missions. "And it came to pass that I beheld that the great mother of abominations did gather together multitudes upon the face of all the earth, among all the nations of the Gentiles, to fight against the Lamb of God. And it came to pass that I, Nephi, beheld the power of the Lamb of God, that it descended upon the saints of the church of the Lamb, and upon the covenant people of the Lord, who were scattered upon all the face of the earth; and *they were armed with righteousness and with the power of God in great glory*."[304]

Drawing upon the perspective of his experiences in escaping from Jerusalem (Babylon), his wilderness journey, and inheriting the promised land (Zion), Nephi recorded this profound insight: "I, Nephi, will show unto you that the tender mercies of the Lord are over all those whom he hath chosen, *because of their faith, to make them mighty even unto the power of deliverance*."[305] Thereafter, he narrates incident after incident in which the power of his covenant with the Lord saved him and his family. The Book of Mormon is a textbook on power in the Covenant.

Alma and Amulek experienced the power of the Covenant as they went forth in faith to minister among the people. When they had been cast into prison and suffered

---

304 1 Nephi 14:14; emphasis added.
305 1 Nephi 1:20; emphasis added.

exceedingly for the sake of Christ, Alma cried unto the Lord for the power of deliverance—a power available because he had made the Covenant, remained faithful to it, and exercised faith in Christ. In an astonishing turn of events, Alma and Amulek broke the cords that bound them—in the same way Nephi broke his cords[306]—and the earth shook until the prison fell and killed the abusers. "And Alma and Amulek came forth out of the prison, and they were not hurt; *for the Lord had granted unto them power, according to their faith which was in Christ.*"[307] Of their ministry, Mormon wrote, "And they had power given unto them, insomuch that they could not be confined in dungeons; neither was it possible that any man could slay them."[308]

Zion people obtain the power of deliverance by abiding in the Covenant!

When Alma had served as leader of the Church for many years and now was instructing his son, Helaman, in the doctrine of the Covenant, he made this observation: "I have been supported under trials and troubles of every kind, yea, and in all manner of afflictions; yea, God has delivered me from prison, and from bonds, and from death; yea, and I do put my trust in him, and he will still deliver me."[309] With perspective, we, too, can look back and point to constant demonstrations of God's power in our lives. Because he and we abide in the Covenant together, we, by our righteousness, are ever in a position to draw upon his power to mitigate life's difficulties. Like the ancient Israelites, we, too, can point to times when we have been delivered from bondage and captivity and our enemies have been neutralized or destroyed. Like Lehi and his family, we, too, by God's everlasting power, have been called out of a wicked environment, and he has delivered us from time to time even down to the present day.[310]

When the circumstances of our lives bind us with seemingly unbreakable bands that only God can break, we, like Alma, should retain in our remembrance our former experiences with the power of God. Because God never changes and because he keeps the Covenant, he will likewise intervene now and in the future, as he has intervened in the past, to help us to face our challenges.[311] Our access to his power is a combination of our righteousness and our faith in Christ. We have confidence that he will not leave us forever bound in cords or held in prison or beaten or despised. We believe that our abiding in the Covenant has summoned his power many times, and our continuing to abide in the Covenant will summon his power of deliverance in the future. Then we, like Alma, can declare that we have been supported under trials and troubles of every kind, and in all manner of afflictions, and that God will yet deliver us from prison, and from bonds, and from death. Therefore, we abide in the Covenant with the assurance that if we continue to put our trust in God, he will manifest his power and deliver us.

---

306 1 Nephi 8:16–18.
307 Alma 14:26–28; emphasis added.
308 Alma 8:31.
309 Alma 36:27.
310 Alma 36:29.
311 Alma 36:28–29.

Section 3   Abide in the Covenant

Other Powers Manifested in the Covenant

Power in the Covenant is manifested in other ways. For example, we enter the Covenant through the ordinance of baptism, which places upon us a name of power—*Jesus Christ*. The power of the name of Jesus Christ is unequaled. During His mortal ministry, Jesus ordained the seventy, gave them power to use his name, and then sent them on missions. He instructed them: "Heal the sick therein, and say unto them, The kingdom of heaven is come nigh unto you [i.e., *We have come with power as authorized servants from the kingdom of heaven and have authority to use the name of Jesus Christ to bless you.*]." When the seventy returned from their missions, they were astonished at the power of the name of Jesus Christ: "And the seventy returned again with joy, saying, Lord, even the devils are subject unto us *through thy name.*"[312] Clearly, the name of Christ is "that ultimate statement of authority."[313]

Concerning the importance of the name of Jesus Christ, the Lord commanded us as Zion people to "take upon you *the name of Christ*. . . . Behold, *Jesus Christ is the name* which is given of the Father, and there is none other name given whereby man can be saved [now or in the future]; . . . for in that name [*Jesus Christ*] shall they be called at the last day."[314] The name of Jesus Christ is a blessing we often overlook. Given to us at baptism, the name of Jesus Christ opens the door to prayer and access to the Father. This power to ask for and receive blessings is one of the supernal powers of the Covenant. Prayer is perhaps most efficacious when it is preceded by sacrifice. Because the vicarious sacrifices we offer in the temple are some of the most Christlike sacrifices—sacrificing for the sake of someone who could not otherwise achieve redemption—the subsequent prayers we offer in the temple often carry added spiritual weight. We cannot quantify the power of prayers offered in the holy temple.

Prayer in the name of Jesus Christ speaks eloquently regarding our relationship with the Lord as it exists in the Covenant. If we would more readily respond to a request from a friend or a family member than we would from a stranger, would not Heavenly Father readily respond to us because we are in the Covenant with him and a member of the family of Jesus Christ? Moreover, if we were to ask a friend or a family member for help in assisting someone of our acquaintance, would they not be willing to respond favorably because of their relationship to us? In like manner, when Zion people, who are of the Covenant, ask Heavenly Father in the name of Jesus Christ to bless people of their acquaintance, he will respond to their request because of their covenant relationship. Because the law of heaven requires asking in the name of Jesus Christ to receive blessings, someone must ask.[315] We believe that it is because of our loving covenantal relationship with the Father that we can ask and he will respond—*because we are family.*

That is the power of the Covenant!

---

312   Luke 10:9, 17; emphasis added.
313   Packer, "An Evening with President Boyd K. Packer," Feb. 29, 2008.
314   D&C 18:21–24; emphasis added.
315   Packer, "Personal Revelation," 59–62.

Safety in the Covenant

Despite its propaganda, Babylon is neither a safe nor a nice place or condition. Those who are foolish enough to reside in Babylon are prone to dangers and adversities without the benefit of armor. The Apostle John calls Babylon a "hold" and a "cage," that is, a prison.[316]

In Babylon, idolatrous people worship other gods, so when trouble strikes, they are left alone to suffer and face overwhelming challenges. The harsh philosophy of Babylon is one that is godless, self-serving, competitive, and lonesome—*anti-Christ*.[317] People in Babylon fare "according to the management of the creature," prosper according to their genius, and conquer according to their strength. They assume no accountability to God, therefore they feel that they can do whatever they please without consequence. In Babylon, they succeed or fail alone. They have a "form of godliness, but they deny the power thereof" (the power of hope in Jesus Christ, the plan of salvation, the holy priesthood, and gifts of the Spirit), and they label the humble followers of Christ as frenzied captives bound by false traditions (ironically, it is the inhabitants of Babylon who are the "frenzied captives"!).[318] When the people of Babylon are faced with trouble, they receive neither aid from Babylon nor respite from her unmerciful and unrelenting attacks. Amazingly, many people insist on living in Babylon and embracing that lifestyle, all the while considering themselves safe.

A scan of the scriptures proves otherwise—in every case! Safety is found *only* in the Covenant. Does that mean a person of the Covenant will not suffer? Of course not. Suffering is part of the testing process for every mortal being. But by abiding in the Covenant, we understand that our afflictions are consecrated for our gain.[319] That is, they are sanctified and therefore changed in purpose. No longer are they merely an adversity; rather, they are counted as a sacrifice—and sacrifice, we are taught, "brings forth the blessings of heaven."[320] Isaiah said, "And though the Lord give you the bread of adversity, and the water of affliction, yet shall not thy teachers be removed into a corner any more, but thine eyes shall see thy teachers."[321] The Bible footnote for the word *teachers* suggests the Savior. Adversity draws the Savior close.

Therefore, when Zion people suffer, they are ultimately safe in the Covenant. Their affliction will not damage them; it will serve to exalt them: "And we know that all things work together for good to them that love God, to them who are the called according to his purpose [his Covenant]."[322] Whereas a noncovenant person suffers for the purpose of leading him to Christ, a covenant person suffers to lead him closer to Christ or sometimes for "Christ's sake."[323] Among other things, this means that Jesus (because we

---

316 Revelation 18:2.
317 Alma 30:12.
318 Alma 30:12–17.
319 2 Nephi 2:2.
320 "Praise to the Man," *Hymns*, no. 27.
321 Isaiah 30:20.
322 Romans 8:28.
323 Alma 4:13; 2 Corinthians 12:10.

are bound to him in the Covenant) will stand beside us, suffer with us, and help us to overcome. In the Covenant, Zion people are never left alone. Thus, it is in the Covenant that our afflictions are consecrated for our eternal welfare. Nephi put it this way: "But behold, I say unto you that ye must pray always, and not faint; that ye must not perform any thing unto the Lord save in the first place ye shall pray unto the Father in the name of Christ, *that he will consecrate thy performance unto thee, that thy performance may be for the welfare of thy soul.*"[324]

In a significant way, safety in the Covenant is linked directly to our active and faithful participation in temple worship. It is in the temple that we receive the blessings of the Covenant in their fulness. Heavenly Father will "establish the people that shall worship" in the temple. If we "honorably hold a name and standing in this thy house,"—that is, if we hold and actively and honorably use a temple recommend—we will be blessed now and "to all generations and for eternity." Great blessings of safety follow: "That no weapon formed against them shall prosper; that he who diggeth a pit for them shall fall into the same himself; that no combination of wickedness shall have power to rise up and prevail over thy people upon whom thy name shall be put in this house; and if any people shall rise against this people, that thine anger be kindled against them; and if they shall smite this people thou wilt smite them; thou wilt fight for thy people as thou didst in the day of battle, that they may be delivered from the hands of all their enemies."[325]

Speaking of the security derived from the law of consecration, as a significant part of the new and everlasting covenant, the Lord said, "Now, this commandment [Covenant] I give unto my servants for their benefit while they remain, for a manifestation of my blessings upon their heads, and for a reward of their diligence *and for their security; for food and for raiment; for an inheritance; for houses and for lands.*"[326]

Clearly, both collectively and individually, we find safety in the Covenant.

Safety through Consecration in the Covenant

Consider that the work and the glory of God are to raise us to immortality at the highest level, called *eternal life.*[327] To that end the Father provides us the Atonement of his Son. The new and everlasting covenant emerges from the Atonement and makes us partners with Jesus in all things, both easy and difficult. By means of the Covenant, we are yoked with the Savior to inseparably face every eventuality. In this relationship, we pledge to each other all that we have and are, and we are therefore entitled to draw upon the resources of the stronger partner for any eventuality. In every way, we are *one* in the Covenant; neither are we divided nor are we alone. Now, because of our covenantal relationship, life's adversities are *consecrated* to the Lord for the welfare of our souls.

---

324   2 Nephi 32:9; emphasis added.
325   D&C 109:24–28.
326   D&C 70:15–16; emphasis added.
327   Moses 1:39.

Consecration is an inclusive law that requires that we consecrate *everything* to the Lord, which by definition would include our difficulties. Think of it this way: When you marry, would you exclude your problems from the vows you make to your spouse? Marriage partners bring everything they have and are to the relationship, and they work through things and make decisions together. Their joint consecration makes them one, and therefore there is no division of resources. They pool everything so that they might face life together. A marriage that does not tolerate the partners' individual problems is not strong and is at risk of failure. But a marriage in which the partners are equally yoked, in which the resources are unselfishly and totally pooled, will survive any storm. So it is with the Lord and us. In the Covenant, we bring all that we have to the relationship, including our problems, and we use the sum of our resources to face life together with the Lord.

That is exactly what the Lord wants. It is by facing difficulties *together* that strong relationships are forged. It is in facing opposition that we discover how deeply loyalties run. As we walk hard roads together, we discover things about each other that we could not learn otherwise. We come to trust and love each other. We find that together we are stronger than when we are apart. We learn to rely on the relationship, and we never want to step away from it. By experience, we discover that in the covenantal relationship, we are absolutely safe. Much like the heat and hammering in the process of forging steel, adversity, becomes an important solidifying agent for that relationship. By means of adversity, the agreement made at the outset of the Covenant by the baptismal ordinance becomes an unbreakable weld. This could be said of the marriage relationship. The *yes* spoken as a vow to form a marriage is only as good as the *yes* spoken as a vow every day thereafter. A marriage would be of little worth if one spouse were to leave the other or let them down. Just so, the Covenant would be of no worth if God were to abandon us and allow us to face trouble alone. President George Q. Cannon said:

> No matter how serious the trial, how deep the distress, how great the affliction, [God] will never desert us. He never has, and He never will. He cannot do it. It is not His character [to do so]. He is an unchangeable being; the same yesterday, the same today, and He will be the same throughout the eternal ages to come. We have found that God. We have made Him our friend, by obeying His Gospel; and He will stand by us. We may pass through the fiery furnace; we may pass through deep waters; but we shall not be consumed nor overwhelmed. We shall emerge from all these trials and difficulties the better and purer for them, if we only trust in our God and keep His commandments.[328]

---

328   Cannon, *Collected Discourses*, 2:185; emphasis added.

The Great Discovery

One of the monumental discoveries of our taking and abiding in the Covenant is this: *God will take care of us.* The Lord's intention is to exalt us in the Covenant, not to destroy us; he uses adversarial situations to build faith rather than to confuse us. He is an omniscient God of consistency, power, mercy, and love. Therefore, in the Covenant with him we are absolutely safe.

One of the greatest demonstrations of the safety of the Covenant is that of the ancient Israelites.

> This is thy God that brought thee up out of Egypt, and had wrought great provocations; yet thou in thy manifold mercies *forsookest them not* in the wilderness: the pillar of the *cloud departed not* from them by day, to lead them in the way; *neither the pillar of fire* by night, to shew them light, and the way wherein they should go. Thou gavest also thy good spirit to *instruct them*, and withheldest not thy *manna* from their mouth, and gavest them *water* for their thirst. *Yea, forty years didst thou sustain them* in the wilderness, [so that] they *lacked nothing;* their *clothes waxed not old, and their feet swelled not.*[329]

The Lord never forsook them, although they were often weak and rebellious. He was with them both day and night. He constantly instructed them. He provided manna and water to sustain them. For four decades of wandering, they lacked nothing! Amazingly, neither their clothing nor their shoes wore out. Perhaps to teach his obstinate children an invaluable lesson, the Lord showed them unmistakably that he could keep them safe in the Covenant.

At the end of Jesus' life, just before he entered Gethsemane, he reminded his Apostles of their early missions when he purposely placed them in a condition of *lack* to teach them of their safety in the Covenant. He accomplished this lesson by sending them out with neither purse nor scrip. Now, looking back, he asked them: "When I sent you without purse, and scrip, and shoes, lacked ye any thing? And they said, Nothing."[330] As much as the Apostles needed firsthand experience with the Covenant's safety, so do we. When we lack, we can go to the Lord, and because we are one with him in the Covenant, he will take care of us. We are safe.

Examples of Safety in the Covenant

Only after the Lord clothed Adam and Eve in skins—skins which represented the protection provided by the Atonement,[331] did he send them into the lone and dreary world, where they were kept safe in the Covenant.

---

329 Nehemiah 9:18–21; emphasis added.
330 Luke 22:35.
331 McConkie and Ostler, *Revelations of the Restoration*, 223.

Lehi abandoned everything to make an extraordinary journey through the harsh wilderness, and he was kept safe in the Covenant. Does safety mean being free from afflictions and adversity? Of course not. Rather, safety in the Covenant suggests that the Lord never leaves us alone. Like the bridegroom who would never leave his suffering wife's side, the Bridegroom, who is our Savior, never leaves us in times of trial. By covenant, he stands beside us, upholds us, cares for us, and loves us to our journey's or trial's end. That is the true safety inherent in the Covenant.

The brother of Jared found safety in the Covenant. After an arduous journey to the seashore, he committed his people into the safekeeping of God and launched eight vessels toward an unknown destination. For 344 days, they were driven forth by a furious wind upon the water. They were tossed and crushed by mountainous waves, buried in the depths of the sea, and cast about by great and terrible tempests—and yet they were safe in the Covenant they had made. "There was no water that could hurt them." The Lord was ever with them: "When they were encompassed about by many waters they did cry unto the Lord, and he did bring them forth again upon the top of the waters. . . . No monster of the sea could break them, neither whale that could mar them; and they did have light continually." They had made the Covenant, and they were safe in it. "And they did sing praises unto the Lord; yea, the brother of Jared did sing praises unto the Lord, and he did thank and praise the Lord all the day long; and when the night came, they did not cease to praise the Lord."[332]

Abraham lay bound upon the altar, but he was safe in the Covenant. The Lord delivered him. His wife was taken from him twice, but she was safe in the Covenant. Abraham prepared to sacrifice Isaac, but he and his son were safe in the Covenant. Even martyrs such as Abinadi and the women and children of Ammonihah were ultimately safe "in the arms of Jesus."[333] Ironically, their safety was defined by martyrdom, which launched them into eternal life. Of course, martyrdom is a manifestation of the sacrifice of all things, which Joseph Smith said was necessary to obtain eternal life.[334] Nevertheless, while they made their sacrifice, they were kept safe in the Covenant. And as we make our sacrifice, the Covenant will keep us safe, too.

Understanding the importance of keeping the Covenant at all costs, Helaman urged the Ammonites to stand firm in their resolve, even when the country was about to be overrun. "But I would not suffer them that they should break this covenant which they had made, supposing that God would strengthen us, insomuch that we should not suffer more because of the fulfilling the oath which they had taken."[335]

Clearly, the best course of action is to keep the Covenant. Mortality is a place of testing and a time to make our sacrifices. But while we are doing so, we gain greater strength and do "not suffer more because of the fulfilling of the oath which [we have] taken."

Lazarus was dead for four days, but he was safe in the Covenant. On that occasion, the Savior focused the attention of Lazarus's sister Martha on Jesus' true identity, saying,

---

332 Ether 6:5–11.
333 Mosiah 13:9; Alma 14:11; Mormon 5:11.
334 Smith, *Lectures on Faith*, 6:7.
335 Alma 56:8.

Section 3   Abide in the Covenant

"I am the resurrection, and the life: he that believeth in me, though he were dead, yet shall he live: *And whosoever liveth and believeth in me shall never die.* Believest thou this?"[336] It is a question that each of us must answer: Do we believe—*really believe*—in this Jesus with whom we have made the Covenant? Will we believe, even with the stark reality of death staring at us, that we are yet safe?

The people of Alma the Elder people escaped their Babylon, made the Covenant with the Lord, and continued to abide in it at every hazard, even when they were in captivity. "And it came to pass that the voice of the Lord came to them in their afflictions, saying: Lift up your heads and be of good comfort, *for I know of the covenant which ye have made unto me; and I will covenant with my people and deliver them out of bondage.*"[337] Alma's people had no misgivings; their faith in the Lord and his Covenant was verified. They were, and always had been, safe in the Covenant.

An incident in Jesus' ministry demonstrates safety in the Covenant. The exhausted Lord set out with his disciples in a boat by night. "And there arose a great storm of wind, and the waves beat into the ship, so that it was now full. And he was in the hinder part of the ship, asleep on a pillow: and they awake him, and say unto him, Master, carest thou not that we perish? And he arose, and rebuked the wind, and said unto the sea, Peace, be still. And the wind ceased, and there was a great calm. And he said unto them, Why are ye so fearful? how is it that ye have no faith?"[338] The Lord's question feels like a rebuke. He might have said, "We have entered the Covenant together, haven't we? That means that I am with you—*always.* Why, then, are you afraid? Where is your faith? Don't you know yet who I am and what to expect of me? We are in this together. You are safe in the Covenant."

Finally, consider the stripling warriors. These were young men who had taken the Covenant and who were suddenly thrust into a new and dangerous environment that required enormous faith. "They never had fought, yet they did not fear death." How had they achieved this level of courage? Helaman described their bravery as the greatest he had ever seen among the Nephites. They had learned it at their mothers' knees. Evidently the concept of safety in the Covenant had been drilled into them so well that they "did not doubt [that] God would deliver them." When Helaman asked them, "What say ye, my sons, will ye go against [the Lamanites] to battle?" they answered, "Father, behold our God is with us, and he will not suffer that we should fall; then let us go forth." They knew who the Lord was, and their faith was in the power and safety of the Covenant: "And they rehearsed unto me the words of their mothers, saying: We do not doubt our mothers knew it." Helaman reported the result: "To my great joy, there had not one soul of them fallen to the earth; yea, and they had fought as if with the strength of God; yea, never were men known to have fought with such miraculous strength."[339] They drew upon the power of God, which was available to them in the Covenant, and they were safe.

---

336   John 11:25–26; emphasis added.
337   Mosiah 24:13; emphasis added.
338   Mark 4:37–40.
339   Alma 56:44–47, 56.

For Zion people, the lesson of safety is of ultimate importance. Only faith that the Lord is near and that he will never leave us can provide sufficient confidence for us to leave Babylon behind, as have other people of great faith, and throw ourselves wholly upon the tender mercies of the Lord. Only faith in the Lord and his promises can help us break from telestial law and embrace celestial law, which makes little sense in a telestial world. But if we will have the courage to sever ourselves from Babylon and allow the Covenant to make of us Zion people, we will make the discovery of a lifetime: We are absolutely safe in the Covenant—safer than we have ever been or felt before.

Progressing in the Covenant

Years of service and purifying exertion are required to prepare us to endure the celestial glory that is typical of Zion. No casual effort will allow us to stand shoulder to shoulder with heavenly beings; our effort must include the totality of our heart, might, mind, and strength. The new and everlasting covenant is designed to snatch us from telestial bondage and complacency, introduce us to celestial law, and fit us for celestial glory.

We begin our progression in the Covenant by duty, which is motivation enough to provide us shelter in the Covenant. Then, keeping the Covenant's associated commandments will hold us firmly on the strait and narrow path. Along the way, as we have experience with the Covenant, we begin to be motivated by understanding; that is, we start to comprehend the reasoning behind the Covenant, and we hunger and thirst for more information. In other words, we now have tasted of the fruit, found it to be delicious, and we desire more. Somewhere along the path, we discover that the Covenant is much more than a set of laws, which seem at times to be restrictive; the Covenant, rather, is a relationship. The Covenant is all about love—love from the Father and the Son. Knowing this, we begin to be motivated by that love. We love God and his Son in return, and our ability to love grows. The more we love God and our fellowmen, the more we become Zion people. Finally, the path of the Covenant we entered into at baptism leads us carefully along until we can stand in the presence of God. But the Covenant does not stop there; the Covenant is an eternal agreement whereby we become like God, inherit all that he has, do all that he does, and have the right to draw upon his resources forever to build our individual kingdoms.

As we examine the Covenant, we see that it begins with general requirements that progressively become more specific. For example, when we are baptized and confirmed, we make broad agreements, one of which is to take upon ourselves the name of Jesus Christ. Later, when we receive the sacrament, we take upon us his name again—this time more specifically—by partaking of the emblems representing his body and blood. Then, as we progress further in the Covenant and receive the covenant of the priesthood, the Lord once again places upon us his name,[340] which allows us to authoritatively do his works. Later still, when we go to the temple to obtain the revelation of the

---

340 Abraham 1:18.

priesthood,[341] we receive, as Brigham Young said, sacred "key words, signs and tokens"[342] that specifically point to Christ and the power of his name.[343] Finally, when we marry for time and eternity and enter into the patriarchal order of the priesthood, we enter the door of exaltation where we receive our spouse in a way that binds us together with a bond that is symbolically as secure as that by which we are bound to the Father and the Son. Now we have taken an essential step in magnifying our primary priesthood calling, the call to eternal life that is stipulated in the oath and covenant of the priesthood.[344] Only by being sealed in marriage can we respond to that call. Only by the marriage covenant can we come to "know the only wise and true God, and Jesus Christ," and experience "eternal lives."[345] Now we have progressed to the point where we are immersed in the Covenant and can truly begin to become like the Father and the Son.

So it is with all our covenants. Initially, we make broad agreements that require general sacrifice and obedience. Then, as we gain understanding about those covenants, we must demonstrate more specific obedience and greater sacrifice. The end result of the process of covenant making is the creation of a celestial person, Zion-like, fully formed in the image of Christ, someone who is willing to be profoundly obedient to every word that proceeds from the mouth of God and to sacrifice anything and everything for him.

Discovering the Relationship through Progression

As we progress in the Covenant, we discover that it is a relationship of equality between two people who love each other. Although this relationship is amazingly *horizontal* rather than *vertical*, we nevertheless covenant to recognize and sustain the lordship of the Savior and the sovereignty of the Father.

Our relationship progresses along lines of intimacy. We enter the Covenant as a servant, we progress to a friend, and we end up as a son or daughter. Joseph Smith set the latter-day example. For example, at the beginning of Joseph's ministry, we hear the Lord referring to him as his servant: "Wherefore, I the Lord, knowing the calamity which should come upon the inhabitants of the earth, called upon *my servant* Joseph Smith, Jun., and spake unto him from heaven, and gave him commandments."[346] Later, we hear the Lord referring to Joseph as his friend: "Verily, I say unto my servant Joseph Smith, Jun., or in other words, I will call you friends, for you are my friends, and ye shall have an inheritance with me."[347] Still later, after Joseph had proved that he would abide in the Covenant at all hazards, we hear the Lord calling him his son: "*My son*, peace be unto thy soul; thine adversity and thine afflictions shall be but a small moment. And then, if thou endure it well, God shall exalt thee on high; thou shalt triumph over all thy foes."[348]

---

341   D&C 2:1.
342   Young, *Discourses of Brigham Young*, 416.
343   Moroni 7:48; 1 John 3:2; D&C 132:24; *Encyclopedia of Mormonism*, 1428.
344   D&C 84:33.
345   D&C 132:34.
346   D&C 1:17; emphasis added.
347   D&C 93:45; emphasis added; D&C 100:1.
348   D&C 121:7–8.

Of course, these titles are somewhat intermixed, but the progression we are speaking of seems to be evident in the Doctrine and Covenants, and these examples serve to illustrate the point.

This pattern—servant-friend-son—might help us to understand our progression in the Covenant. A servant receives and fulfills the commandments of his Lord. A servant might know his Lord, but not intimately.

A friend, on the other hand, because of his relationship with the Lord, is in a position to ask what he can do for the other person. Friends do not command each other; rather, one friend might request something of the other, knowing that his friend will help. Friends share intimate conversations, they know a great deal about each other, and they have much in common. It is worth noting that servants and friends do not necessarily represent eternal relationships, as does a family. The status of servant or friend can be temporary, but always these relationships are defined by set boundaries. Therefore, if we are to progress from servant or friend to family, something significant in the relationship must change. That brings us to the ultimate stage of the Covenant: to become *children of God*.

A child—a son or daughter—is part of the most intimate type of relationship: *family*. A child comes to know everything about his Parent. A child has the right to say to his Parent, "Your name is my name and your work is my work. I am yours forever by covenant; we are linked together by blood; we are bound together by eternal love." While one of the greatest manifestations of love is offering your life for a friend,[349] the ultimate sacrifices are made within the family, which, actually, is the highest level of friendship. There the greatest loyalties are forged. We enter the Covenant to serve the Lord, become his intimate friend, and become his child to whom he bequeaths all that he has. "Marvel not that all mankind, yea, men and women, all nations, kindreds, tongues and people, must be born again; yea, born of God, changed from their carnal and fallen state, to a state of righteousness, being redeemed of God, *becoming his sons and daughters*."[350] Zion people walk and talk with their Father and Brother and enjoy their familial relationship.[351]

Order in the Covenant

Having received the Covenant, Frederick G. Williams, a close associate of Joseph Smith, faltered in his agreement. The result, as is always the case, was that Satan gained power over him. In a merciful rebuke, the Lord called him back to the safety of the Covenant: "I have commanded you to bring up your children in light and truth. But verily I say unto you, my servant Frederick G. Williams, you have continued under this condemnation; you have not taught your children light and truth, according to the commandments; *and that wicked one hath power, as yet, over you, and this is the cause of your affliction. And now a commandment I give unto you—if you will be delivered you shall set in order your own house,* for there are many things that are not right in your house."[352]

---

349 John 15:13.
350 Mosiah 27:25; emphasis added.
351 Moses 7:21.
352 D&C 93:40–43; emphasis added.

Zion is defined by order, and order defines the lives of Zion people. As much as the Covenant brings power and safety into our lives, the Covenant also brings order—the order of Zion. The covenant-making opportunities in our lives are like compass points that keep us oriented to true north. By giving strict diligence to the ordinances and covenants, we invite the Lord's order into our lives. Repeatedly, the Lord reminds us that his house is an ordered house: "Behold, mine house is a house of order, saith the Lord God, and not a house of confusion."[353] Therefore, he commands us to organize ourselves against the standard of the Covenant so that we might remain safe and clean: "And I give unto you, who are the first laborers in this last kingdom, a commandment that you assemble yourselves together, *and organize yourselves,* and prepare yourselves, and sanctify yourselves; yea, purify your hearts, and cleanse your hands and your feet before me, that I may make you clean."[354] This quality of order and its associated blessings can be accomplished and found only by and through the Covenant.

Order and Ordinances

The words *order, ordain,* and *ordinance* come from the same root. Ordinances give order to the Covenant; likewise, ordinances provide order in our lives. The order of salvation is an order of authorized *ordinances.* Ordinances are the markers that define the path leading to eternal life. Is there any other way to achieve exaltation? No. Jesus said, "My house is a house of order."[355] To Peter and the Apostles, he said, "Go ye into all the world, and preach the gospel to every creature. He that believeth and is baptized shall be saved; but he that believeth not shall be damned."[356] Without authorized ordinances there is no possibility of salvation.

The importance of ordinances seems like nonsense to many in the world. The Lord uses sacred symbols and rites to teach us about *his* world. To access the powers associated with these ordinances, we must make agreements or covenants with the Lord. When we keep our part of the agreement, he keeps his. Then we progress in an orderly manner, ordinance to ordinance, blessing to blessing, power to power, knowledge to knowledge, until we become like God.

We must receive the ordinances in the correct order; otherwise, they lack power to save. The Apostle Paul was teaching in the province of Ephesus when he met a group of twelve disciples who said they had been baptized. He wondered about this and asked them if they had received the Holy Ghost. They had not. Joseph Smith said you might as well baptize a bag of sand as baptize without conferring the Holy Ghost—one without the other is meaningless.[357] Paul asked these people how they had been baptized, and they said they had received John's baptism. We might speculate on what they meant, but obviously they had not received the ordinances correctly. Perhaps they had received a baptism from an unauthorized person after the pattern or in the name of John the Baptist. In any case, Paul

---

353 D&C 132:8, 18; 88:119; 109:8.
354 D&C 88:74; emphasis added.
355 D&C 132:8.
356 Mark 16:15–16.
357 Smith, *Teachings of the Prophet Joseph Smith,* 314.

explained to them that baptisms must be done in the name of Jesus Christ by someone having the authority of Jesus Christ. That is the order of this ordinance. Because Paul had authority to baptize correctly, he baptized them *again* the right way, and then he conferred upon them the gift of the Holy Ghost. Now they were on the ordained path.

What do we learn from this account? Being good is not enough to save us, nor is merely having good intentions. We must be good and do the right thing in the right order if we want to end up in the right place. We should keep in mind that the people Paul was teaching were sincere people who were trying to live good lives, but they had a mistaken idea. When Paul, who was authorized by Jesus Christ, performed the ordinance of baptism correctly, these people suddenly received the promised blessings associated with true baptism and the Holy Ghost, and miraculous things began to happen: "And when Paul had laid [his] hands upon them, the Holy Ghost came on them; and they spake with tongues, and prophesied."[358] Miracles always happen as a result of receiving covenants and ordinances. These miracles are signs that the ordinances are true. Zion people order their lives according to the ordinances; they follow the ordained markers leading to eternal life, and they experience miracle after miracle along the way.

Order and Consecration

The issue of order goes to the heart of the new and everlasting covenant: *the law of consecration*. This culminating law bids us to acknowledge that all things belong to God. We are stewards[359] who are accountable to him for the discharge of our stewardships.[360] What is done with his property is not ours to dictate—it is his. The element of order mandated by consecration insists that we esteem others as ourselves[361] in order that all men and women might be made equal according to their wants, needs, family situations, and access to the Lord's storehouse.[362]

This is the established order of the law of consecration as dictated by the Covenant. When we ignore, rationalize, or modify this order to fit our personal objectives, we step away from the Covenant and become a law unto ourselves.[363] That attitude opens the door for Satan to afflict us. Then we, like Frederick G. Williams, might also receive the Lord's rebuke. But if we will allow the Covenant to help us organize ourselves and set our houses in order, we will reap power, safety, and prosperity in the order of the Covenant.

Abide in the Covenant

We began by quoting the Lord's requirement of those who have received the Covenant: "I have decreed in my heart, saith the Lord, that I will prove you in all things, whether you will abide in my covenant, even unto death, that you may be found worthy. For if

---

358   Acts 19:1–7.
359   D&C 38:17; 104:11–14.
360   D&C 72:3; 104:13–18.
361   D&C 38:24–27; 51:3, 9; 70:14; 78:6; 82:17.
362   D&C 51:3.
363   D&C 88:21–35.

ye will not abide in my covenant ye are not worthy of me."[364] Our access to power, our safety, our progression, and our future glory pivot on our abiding (staying put) in the Covenant. The Covenant secures us to Jesus Christ, the True Vine, from whom we, the branches, receive life and sustaining nourishment. Jesus taught:

> I am the true vine, and my Father is the husbandman.
> Every branch in me that beareth not fruit he taketh away: and every branch that beareth fruit, he purgeth it, that it may bring forth more fruit.
> Now ye are clean through the word which I have spoken unto you.
> Abide in me, and I in you. As the branch cannot bear fruit of itself, except it abide in the vine; no more can ye, except ye abide in me.
> I am the vine, ye are the branches: He that abideth in me, and I in him, the same bringeth forth much fruit: for without me ye can do nothing.
> If a man abide not in me, he is cast forth as a branch, and is withered; and men gather them, and cast them into the fire, and they are burned.
> If ye abide in me, and my words abide in you, ye shall ask what ye will, and it shall be done unto you.
> Herein is my Father glorified, that ye bear much fruit; so shall ye be my disciples.[365]

Notice that the branches are already producing when the husbandman (God) comes, but he wants them to produce at a higher level. Therefore, he begins to prune, that is, to "purge and purify." With regard to the Covenant made between the Husbandman and the branches, purging and purifying is exactly what each party agreed must happen. The branches (we) agreed to endure (abide) the Husbandman's purging and purifying process with the assurance that we would progressively gain greater strength and produce more fruit. With that goal in mind, the Husbandman begins to cut away from the branches anything that saps their strength. He carefully directs the new growth so that the branches might perform optimally. For a period of time, the branches may appear (and probably feel) pitiful and barren. For a season, they may not produce much fruit. But the Husbandman knows that in time the purging and purifying procedure will cause the branches to mature and bring forth more than they ever have before.

Returning to the Lord's commandment—"abide in my covenant"—we see the two meanings of *abide* represented in the purging and purifying process: (1) the branches must *remain* attached to the True Vine for the duration of the process; (2) the branches

---

364 D&C 98:14–15.
365 John 15:1–8.

must *endure* the husbandman's purging and purifying efforts. Sometimes this procedure is called *chastening*. "For whom the Lord loveth he chasteneth, and scourgeth every son whom he receiveth. If ye endure chastening, God dealeth with you as with sons; for what son is he whom the father chasteneth not?" In this case, to chasten means "to make chaste"[366] or to purify. "Now no chastening for the present seemeth to be joyous, but grievous: nevertheless afterward it yieldeth the peaceable fruit of righteousness unto them which are exercised thereby."[367] "Without sufferings [chastisement]," we are reminded, "[we] could not be made perfect."[368]

Abiding in the Covenant Summons Divine Love

Our faithfulness in abiding in the Covenant directly affects our ability to draw upon the Savior's love. Jesus said, "If ye keep my commandments, ye shall abide in my love."[369] The stated reward is remarkable: "Ye shall ask what ye will, and it shall be done unto you."[370] We will never lack for nourishment or strength if we (the branches) abide in Christ (the True Vine), and if we will endure the purging and purifying process. To lack nothing is a central principle of Zion. Our determination to remain unfailingly attached to the True Vine allows us the covenantal right to ask for blessings and to receive accordingly.

Abiding in the Covenant disproportionately rewards the sacrifice that we make to remain and endure. King Benjamin reminded us that God's blessings always exceed our efforts in faithfulness: "If ye should serve him with all your whole souls yet ye would be unprofitable servants."[371] Eternal law states that God cannot be in debt or beholden to anyone; we are always in debt to him. King Benjamin illustrated this truism by pointing out that God blesses us with our lives and supports us from moment to moment—indebtedness that we can never repay. Beyond life and support, he has also blessed us with the Atonement and the Covenant. By means of the Covenant, he has blessed us by revealing his lifestyle—his commandments. When we obey his commandments, he rewards us immediately, which creates an even greater imbalance in his favor: "And ye are still indebted unto him, and are, and will be, forever and ever."[372] Hence, by abiding in the Covenant we learn that there is risk neither in trusting him nor in sacrificing to obey him. We are always blessed in excess of our sacrifice.

Beyond receiving abundant blessings, abiding in the Covenant also defines the relationship between us and the Lord, which is founded on love. Blessings flow to us in this covenantal relationship. Just as a loving husband showers his wife with gifts of affection, so God generously and voluntarily showers us with blessings that speak of his love for us—indisputable evidences of his affection.

---

366 *Encyclopedia of Mormonism*, 264.
367 Hebrews 12:6–7, 11.
368 JST, Hebrews 11:40.
369 John 15:10.
370 John 15:8.
371 Mosiah 2:21.
372 Mosiah 2:22–24.

Blessings are also a means by which God and man are reconciled through the Atonement of Jesus Christ. Moreover, blessings comfort the righteous[373] and lift the hearts of the oppressed.[374] Blessings describe the Lord's devotion to the Covenant and his gratitude for our likewise abiding in it. Blessings reveal the Lord's perfect set of attributes and characteristics, including his power, his awareness, and his love, all of which he consecrates to us in the Covenant. Blessings attest to his nearness and his interest in our welfare. They communicate, "I am aware. I am near. I love you." Blessings anchor us to our hope in Christ, which strengthens us to continue to abide in the Covenant until we have arrived at its exalted destination. Blessings communicate that we are never alone; in the Covenant that would simply be impossible.

Abiding in the Covenant through the Sacrament

As mentioned previously, one way that we abide in the Covenant is through the covenant of the sacrament. By means of this singular ordinance, we "retain a remission of sins"[375] and "remember, and always retain in remembrance, the greatness of God."[376]

The sacrament allows us to renew our baptismal covenant by worthily partaking of "the emblems of the flesh and blood of Christ."[377] Once again, we agree to (1) take upon ourselves the name of Jesus Christ; (2) always remember him, his Atonement, his teachings, his example, and his love for us; and (3) keep all the agreements that we made at baptism, including every commandment of God, and "to live by every word that proceedeth forth from the mouth of God."[378] The sacrament is significant in that it assures us a continuing remission of our sins, which is essential for pure-hearted Zion people.

It is by the ordinance of the sacrament that we receive the assurance of our retaining the gift of the Holy Ghost, which we were commanded to receive at baptism. Always having the Lord's Spirit with us is the Lord's sign to us that we are yet retaining a remission of sins by the merits of Jesus Christ.[379] This allows us imperfect beings to progress in the Covenant until we become Zion-like and receive the ultimate promise concerning the sacramental covenant: eternal life. Elder McConkie wrote: "As his part of the contract, the Lord covenants: 1. That such worthy saints shall have his Spirit to be with them; and 2. That in due course they shall inherit eternal life."[380]

Summary and Conclusion

The new and everlasting covenant is the first pillar upon which Zion is built. The Covenant is the most glorious ever revealed. It contains the greatest hope and the most impres-

---

373 Daniel 9:4.
374 Psalms 74:20–21.
375 Mosiah 4:12; JST, Matthew 26:22–25; JST, Mark 14:20–25; JST, Luke 22:17–20.
376 Mosiah 4:12.
377 D&C 20:40.
378 McConkie, *Mormon Doctrine,* 660; D&C 84:44.
379 2 Nephi 31:19; Moroni 6:4; D&C 3:20.
380 John 6:5–4; McConkie, *Mormon Doctrine,* 660.

sive promises of anything found on earth or in heaven. By abiding its terms we can escape Babylon, flee to Zion, and forever abide safely in the embrace of our Eternal Father.

The Father himself created the new and everlasting covenant for the salvation of his children.[381] The purposes of the Covenant are to provide us: (1) knowledge and power for personal salvation, and (2) knowledge, authority, and power to help save other people by offering and administering to them the Covenant. Our ability to become Zion people—and even our entire eternal future—hang upon our diligence in adhering to the terms of the Covenant. The Lord said, "I have decreed in my heart, saith the Lord, that I will prove you in all things, whether you will abide in my covenant, even unto death, that you may be found worthy. For if ye will not abide in my covenant ye are not worthy of me."[382]

The deeper we dig into the doctrine of the Covenant, the more we discover a loving relationship. A caring Father is offering us all that he has and is. Therefore, he reveals to us the laws by which he lives, and the same eternal covenants of progression and exaltation that made him who he is. He offers these to us knowing that the Covenant will help us to grow from dependence to independence, from natural men to gods.

To make our relationship *sure*, and, furthermore, to insure the terms of the Covenant, three distinct offerings must be made: (1) The Father offers to share with us the supernal blessings of the Covenant; (2) the Son offers to cover the infinite expenses of the Covenant that we cannot meet; and (3) we offer our hearts. Yielding our hearts to God allows us to be assimilated into the celestial order of the gods. We do this by living the celestial laws of Zion in a telestial world, adopting the Father's work of redemption as our own, and becoming experts at serving and saving his children.

The Covenant contains multiple benefits and powers. For example, because it is the word of God, the Covenant has the inherent power of *leavening*. Its doctrines grow within us until we are totally leavened by them. The doctrines of the Covenant transform us into Zion people.

The Covenant separates us from the world. When we enter into the Covenant by baptism, we are *born again* into a new life.[383] We *die* as to our old life and are *born* again as new beings with a new father, Jesus Christ; we have a new family, the Church of Jesus Christ.[384] Now we are his covenant people. As such, we will be forever separate and unique, the Lord's peculiar treasure.[385]

There is power in the Covenant. As we enter the Covenant through baptism, the Lord places upon us his name, which is a name of power—*Jesus Christ*. Through that name, because we are now in a loving covenantal relationship, we can ask the Father for blessings by the power of the name of Jesus Christ, and God will respond—*because we are family.*

---

381 3 Nephi 16:5; 20:12, 25, 27, 29, 46; 21:4, 7; 29:1; Mormon 5:14; 9:47; Ether 4:15; Moroni 10:33; D&C 84:40.
382 D&C 98:14–15.
383 Mosiah 27:25; Alma 7:14; Moses 6:59; John 3:3–7.
384 Moses 5:7.
385 Exodus 19:5; Psalms 135:4.

Section 3   Abide in the Covenant

There is safety in the Covenant. Because Babylon is a dangerous condition, we seek the Lord's safety. This can be found only in the Covenant. When we finally garner the courage to abandon the telestial condition and embrace celestial law, which we must do in order to become Zion-like, we will make the discovery of a lifetime: We are absolutely safe—safer than we have ever been or felt before! Safety in the Covenant also applies to the afflictions that we suffer in mortality. When we suffer, our afflictions are consecrated for our gain *in the Covenant*.[386] The Lord converts our afflictions from destructive to exalting: "And we know that all things work together for good to them that love God, to them who are the called according to his purpose [his Covenant]."[387]

The Covenant *orders* our lives so that we might progress to eternal life. As order applies to progression, we initially obey the laws of the Covenant out of a sense of duty. Over time, duty progresses to understanding, and ultimately we are motivated to obey because of love. Step by step, as we progress in the Covenant with each higher law and ordinance, general requirements become more specific. Likewise, we progress in the Covenant from servant to friend to a son or daughter of God.

Living within the order of the Covenant protects us from the wicked one, while disorder, or disobedience, gives Satan power to afflict us. Therefore, the Lord commands us to set our houses in order according to the stipulations of the Covenant.

The order available to us through living the laws and ordinances of the Covenant keeps the compass of our lives oriented toward true north. The Lord reminds us that his house is a house of order and not of confusion. We progress to eternal life by following the ordained path. This path has markers, or ordinances, which define the order of the Covenant. Each ordinance must be received in its proper order and lived faithfully if eternal life is to be gained. There is no other way. Without authorized ordinances there is no possibility of salvation.

The order of the Covenant and the law of consecration go hand in hand. The Lord's claim to the resources of the earth supersedes our claims. This is the covenantal order. No longer can we consider ourselves as owners but rather as accountable stewards of the Lord's property. Moreover, the covenantal order of relationships is one of equality, esteeming all men and women as ourselves and seeking for unity and cooperation. We cannot achieve the necessary faith to live the law of consecration without the ordering power of the priesthood and the Covenant's additional covenants and ordinances. But if we will allow the Covenant to help us to order our houses and lives, we will reap power, safety, and prosperity, according to the order of the Covenant.

"Abide in the Covenant" is the commandment of the Lord. Our ability to access power, find safety, progress, and attain future glory hinge on our abiding (staying put) in the Covenant. The Covenant secures us to Jesus Christ, the True Vine, from whom we, the branches, receive life and sustaining nourishment. In the Vine, the Husbandman, by covenant, purges and purifies us to fit us for eternal life.

---

386   2 Nephi 2:2.
387   Romans 8:28.

Our faithfulness in abiding in the Covenant directly affects our ability to use the name of Jesus Christ. By this name of power, which we receive the right to use at baptism, we can approach the Father and ask for and receive blessings. Because the Father and the Son promise to respond, we never need to experience lack; sufficiency and abundance are central principles of Zion.

Our receiving the Father's blessings speaks to a covenantal relationship founded on love. His blessings anchor us to our hope in Christ and communicate that we are never alone. Because of God's blessings, we are always indebted to him—an incredible benefit understood only by those who abide faithfully in the Covenant.

These are the blessings of the Covenant and the condition of Zion people.

Section 4
The New and Everlasting Covenant—The Holy Marriage

Throughout the scriptures, the marriage metaphor is used to describe our covenantal relationship with the Lord. He is the Bridegroom,[388] and the Church is the bride.[389] By extension, we, individually, are his bride: "For as a young man marrieth a virgin, so shall thy sons marry thee: and as the bridegroom rejoiceth over the bride, so shall thy God rejoice over thee."[390] We are to prepare ourselves for the time the Bridegroom comes to receive us: "Wherefore, be faithful, praying always, having your lamps trimmed and burning, and oil with you, that you may be ready at the coming of the Bridegroom—For behold, verily, verily, I say unto you, that I come quickly."[391] We are to become prepared and "beautiful" for him: "adorned as a bride."[392]

That the Lord chose marriage to describe the new and everlasting covenant should summon our solemn contemplation. Marriage is the summit of gospel covenants, the relationship that is the most intimate, most enduring, and the most loving of unions. Marriage is the relationship in which is manifest the power of God to create; children spring from this union; multiplication, replenishment, and fruitfulness become possible. The metaphor of marriage suggests profound loyalty, the abandonment of selfish interests, and complete sacrifice. Marriage requires the consecration of one's time, talents, and resources to his or her companion, the sum of what one is and has. Marriage is a covenantal lifestyle that results in *oneness*, a relationship wherein the partners are no longer "twain, but one flesh," joined together by God and intended to endure beyond man's attempts to put asunder.[393]

If marriage is to be successful, it requires losing one's life in selfless service to and the loving of one's spouse; then, in return, marriage leads to finding one's life in a more

---

388   Matthew 9:15; Mark 2:19; Luke 5:34; John 3:29.
389   Revelation 21:2, 9–10; 22:17.
390   Isaiah 62:5.
391   D&C 33:17; see also D&C 88:92; 133:10, 19.
392   D&C 109:74.
393   Matthew 19:6.

exalted purpose.[394] Marriage urges the best of behavior in the partners. Think of what we would say of our "marriage" to the Lord: "and they shall mention the loving kindness of their Lord, and all that he has bestowed upon them according to his goodness, and according to his loving kindness, forever and ever."[395] Marriage is *being yoked* together to ease one another's burdens,[396] and the mutual sharing of each other's challenges: "In all their afflictions he was afflicted . . . ; and in his love, and in his pity, he redeemed them, and bore them, and carried them all the days."[397] By purpose and by design marriage is eternal,[398] the highest order of celestial living,[399] the ultimate source of happiness,[400] and significantly the highest order of the priesthood.[401] Conversely, disloyalty to the marriage covenant is a grievous sin, "most abominable above all sins save it be the shedding of innocent blood or denying the Holy Ghost."[402] Clearly, the Lord takes seriously the new and everlasting covenant and expects us to do the same.

In the foreword of Donna B. Nielsen's excellent work, *The Beloved Bridegroom*, Dr. Robert J. Norman wrote: "The wedding ceremony was a metaphor often used by Christ and the Old Testament authors. A study of the Jewish marriage customs yields a wealth of spiritual understanding and deeper insight into the teachings of Jesus and the Biblical prophets."[403] Donna Nielsen explained: "A knowledge of Biblical marriage imagery can greatly enrich our understanding of how God relates to us through covenants. Biblical covenant marriage imagery encompasses principles as diverse as Sabbath observance, the Atonement, temple worship, and missionary work. It literally begins with Adam and ends with Zion."[404] Let us, therefore, examine the new and everlasting covenant by contrasting it with the Jewish marriage tradition. In advance, we thank Donna B. Nielsen for her generous support in providing us access to her research.

Born to Marry

Elder John A. Widtsoe stated that marriage is "the most important event between birth and death,"[405] and certainly the Jewish people agreed. We cannot overstate the importance of marriage in Jewish society. Marriage was clearly linked to the covenant God made with Israel; in fact, we might say that it was understood that children were born with the purpose of marrying. Donna Nielsen stated that an infant male "was often affectionately called 'the little bridegroom.' This reflected one of three great hopes that parents had for their children, namely that their children would study Torah [study the scriptures], be under the wedding canopy [marry in the covenant], and do good deeds

---

394 Matthew 10:39.
395 D&C 133:52.
396 Matthew 11:30.
397 D&C 133:53.
398 D&C 132:19.
399 D&C 131:2.
400 McKay, *Man May Know for Himself*, 235.
401 McConkie, *Mormon Doctrine*, 559.
402 Alma 39:5.
403 Nielsen, *Beloved Bridegroom*, iii.
404 Nielsen, *Beloved Bridegroom*, 2.
405 Widtsoe, *Evidences and Reconciliations*, 297.

[live righteous lives]."[406] Immediately we see the connection between marriage and the new and everlasting covenant. And so with us, if we understand the symbolism, from the moment of birth, our life's purpose should be to learn about and prepare for the Bridegroom, enter into a Covenant with the Bridegroom, and do the works of the Bridegroom. As much as Jewish children were born to marry, we are born to enter into the Covenant.

Because marriage was *the* goal of Jewish life, husbands and wives married at an early age. No later than eighteen was the norm, and most often they married years before that. A boy became a Son of the Law by age thirteen, and technically one month later he was considered of marriageable age. Girls were eligible at twelve years and one month.[407] In today's culture, we might have difficulty imagining Joseph and Mary, two teenagers, taking on the heavy responsibility of marriage and caring for the Savior of the world. Also, we might struggle with the concept that Jesus could have been married for twelve to fifteen years and had children before he began his ministry at age thirty. But, according to Jewish custom, this may have been true. Marriage was the focal point of Jewish life, and we might imagine that Joseph and Mary followed the prevailing tradition by marrying in their teens.

The Parents' Responsibility and the Bride's Choice

Marriages were thought to be too important to be left to chance. Fathers and mothers made these decisions for their children. Who else loved the child more? Who else had the child's best interests in mind? Who else wanted the child's happiness more than the parents? Today, we might cringe at this ancient custom, but Jewish children expected their parents to advocate for their happiness. Despite the fact that the parents were expected to prayerfully deliberate, then introduce their child to the intended spouse, the child owned the ultimate choice. Their agency was never violated.

Today, of course, parents do not formally choose their children's mates, but the similarity between the Covenant and the ancient custom is clear: Parents have the responsibility to introduce their children to Christ. Fathers, by virtue of holding the priesthood, have the responsibility to take their children into the waters of baptism and help them to enter into the new and everlasting covenant with Jesus. Now the children are given over, or "married," to Christ by covenant, and, taking upon them his name, they begin a relationship with him that will end up in the mansions of his Father.[408]

Love for each other was expected to be cultivated after the marriage, not necessarily before.[409] We note that after Isaac married Rebekah he grew in his love for her.[410] This reversal of order might seem strange to us, but the implication is intriguing: Covenant people grow together in love as they remain true to each other. When we enter into the new and everlasting covenant, we do so without a full appreciation for or love of the

---

406   Nielsen, *Beloved Bridegroom*, 4.
407   Nielsen, *Beloved Bridegroom*, 2.
408   Enos 1:27; Ether 12:32–37; D&C 59:2; 98:18.
409   Nielsen, *Beloved Bridegroom*, 13.
410   Genesis 24:67.

Lord. These things take time. But as we live together in the Covenant and as we have experience with the Lord, we grow to love him more and more. "The Semitic root word for 'love' is *haw* or *hav*. It means 'to warm' or 'to kindle,' 'to set on fire.'"[411] Over time, our love for the Bridegroom grows from an ember to a blazing fire until that love becomes as perfect as the God of love,[412] who "dwells in everlasting burnings."[413]

Requirements to Legalize the Covenant

The marriage covenant "had serious implications. There were three parts that were vital to a completed marriage contract in biblical times. These were *money, writ*, and *intercourse*. All three of these conditions had to be met for a marriage to be recognized as legal." The groom was expected to pay a *bride price* for his beloved. Then he was to offer her a marriage contract, a *writ* or *ketuba*, whereby he consecrated himself to his bride. Finally, the marriage had to be consummated; he must *know* his wife through *sexual relations*. This last condition fulfilled the requirement that blood be shed to complete the covenant.[414]

Thus, in comparing marriage to the new and everlasting covenant, we (the bride) are:
1. "Bought with a price."[415]
2. United by covenant according to the law of consecration, which is "the law of the celestial kingdom."[416]
3. *Known*, or "made perfect through Jesus the mediator of the new covenant, who wrought out this perfect atonement through the shedding of his own blood."[417]

When we consider these conditions, we begin to understand the price that Jesus was willing to pay to draw us to him, redeem us, and secure our eternal affections. Marvin Wilson wrote: "The joining of a man and a woman is a reenactment or replica of God's eternal covenant relation to his chosen. To understand Biblical marriage is to understand the Biblical concept of covenant. In Hebrew 'to make a covenant' is literally 'to cut a covenant.' . . . The shedding of blood [in the sacrifice of an animal] dramatically ratified and sealed the covenant (Genesis 15:9–18; Jeremiah 34:18–20). If one attempted to break the covenant, the blood served as a powerful visual lesson that one's own blood would be shed. In brief, it was a solemn oath to be kept on pain of death. It was thus inviolable and irrevocable."[418]

Initiating the Marriage Proposal

The bridegroom initiated the offering of the covenant of marriage to the bride. When we consider this action in light of the new and everlasting covenant, we see something ten-

---

411 Nielsen, *Beloved Bridegroom*, 13.
412 1 John 4:8.
413 Isaiah 33:14–15.
414 Nielsen, *Beloved Bridegroom*, 18.
415 1 Corinthians 6:20.
416 D&C 105:4.
417 D&C 76:69.
418 Wilson, *Our Father Abraham*, 205.

der and loving about the character of the Savior. We are immediately impressed by the fact that he, not we, invites us into the new and everlasting covenant. Clearly, "we love him, because he first loved us."[419] We often miss the fact that when we are baptized, Jesus is the one who reached out to us and bade us enter into an eternal covenantal relationship with him. We sometimes mistakenly think that we were the ones who instigated the process, but, using the comparisons with the Jewish marriage tradition, that is not true. In advance of every baptism is Jesus' implied invitation. This fact speaks to his adoring love for us. He is the Bridegroom, and we are his potential bride. He is the one who begins the covenant-making process. He does this through the Holy Ghost and through his authorized representatives: fathers, home teachers, bishops, or missionaries.

The marriage proposal often took place at the harvest season, suggesting a bounteous relationship and a fruitful future.[420] Likewise, when we join with the Lord in the Covenant, we glorify both him and his Father and we "bear much fruit" together.[421] The proposal procedure began with the bridegroom going to the house of the bride. He was accompanied by his father or a close friend or friends. We can envision a small entourage, a companionship, two or more witnesses (like missionary companions), on an important mission to convey an invitation of infinite worth to the intended bride. In her presence, the bridegroom would make the covenantal offer while his friends supported him and bore witness of the event. This was the beginning of a union of holiness, for, truly, upon her acceptance of the marriage covenant, the bride would effectively ascribe holiness unto the lord,[422] her new husband. Donna Nielsen wrote: "The collective term for all that broadly comprises a Jewish marriage is *Kiddushin*, which literally means 'sanctities.' This concept includes the ideas of being *devoted irrevocably*, being *sanctified and set apart*, and being *consecrated*."[423] Clearly, the Jewish marriage is the perfect metaphor for the new and everlasting covenant.

Entering into the Covenant

The Bridegroom's proposal to us includes sacred rituals that *consecrate* him to us (the bride), and our accepting his proposal consecrates us to him. We hear overtures of the law of consecration in this. Other symbolisms of the new and everlasting covenant become evident as the betrothal ceremony unfolds. In the ancient Jewish marriage, the groom offered the bride's father a "bride price"—she was "bought with a price."[424] Then the bridegroom presented his potential bride a written covenant of marriage that he had prepared. He also offered her a "gift of value," which represented a "token" of his promise and an "emblem" of his love. With the token he recited a pledge to irrevocably bind and consecrate (dedicate) himself to her forever. Then, in the presence of two witnesses, he placed before his beloved a cup of wine. If she drank of the cup, the contract of marriage

---

419   1 John 4:19.
420   Nielsen, *Beloved Bridegroom*, 14.
421   John 15:8.
422   Exodus 39:30.
423   Nielsen, *Beloved Bridegroom*, 18.
424   1 Corinthians 6:20.

was ratified or sealed, and the betrothal period began. Moreover, by drinking of the cup, she indicated her willingness to take upon herself her husband's name. At that point, the couple, along with their guests, shared a covenantal meal.

Thus, by these rituals that were rich in imagery, the bridegroom and bride entered into the eternal covenant of marriage. When the ceremony was complete, the only question that remained was whether or not the rituals that represented the Covenant would translate into lifelong acts of devotion and consecration. That is, would the covenant become *enduring* by the couple's subsequent loyalty, patience, sacrifice, and love? Or would the covenant remain a set of symbols and a piece of paper upon which promises had been made but never enacted?

Now let us examine the symbolism of laws, rites, and ordinances[425] of the Jewish betrothal period and marriage.

Bought with a Price

When the marriage delegation, which included the groom, his father, his friends, and witnesses, arrived at the bride's home, the proposal ceremony began. First, the young man paid the girl's father a "bride price." There are several important symbolic parallels to our covenant with the Savior portrayed in the price bridegroom paid for the bride. "It meant a pledge of money given by the man to seal his offer to marry. This was not like buying a slave but was perceived as compensating the father for the great loss of his daughter and her contribution to the household. It recognized the care and diligence required to raise her to be a suitable wife. In addition, it also sealed a bond of alliance between the two families."[426] This relationship of *ownership* is described in the word *segulah*, "which means 'peculiar treasure' or 'treasured relationship.' . . . Truly, the worth of a bride was great in the eyes of her husband."[427]

Importantly, the bride price "signified the transfer of authority from father to husband."[428] That is, when the bride gave her consent and entered into the covenant, she agreed to fully belong to her husband, not as if she were a slave or property, but that their relationship would be *exclusive* as that of a beloved eternal companion. She was "bought with a price."[429] Now she was expected to shift her loyalty from her father to her husband and follow him in righteousness.

Of great significance was the amount of the bride price. A small amount suggested that her husband held her in low esteem and of little value. But if he paid a great deal for her in money or service, the implication was that he was acquiring something extremely valuable that required cherishing.[430] Thus, a bridegroom consecrating his all to "purchase" his bride would signify both immense sacrifice and unbounded love. It showed

---

425 Lundwall, *Temples of the Most High*, 87.
426 Nielsen, *Beloved Bridegroom*, 21.
427 Nielsen, *Beloved Bridegroom*, 25–26.
428 Nielsen, *Beloved Bridegroom*, 21, referencing John J. Collins, "Marriage, Divorce, and Family in Second Temple Judaism," 104–62.
429 1 Corinthians 7:23.
430 Nielsen, *Beloved Bridegroom*, 22.

that, in his eyes, she was of infinite worth. We recall that Jacob "served seven years for Rachel, and they seemed to him but a few days because of his love for her."[431] When we consider the bride price, we cannot avoid the reference to the Savior, who paid for us with his life and offers us all that he is and has. He bought us with "his own blood."[432]

Although the bride's father received the bride price, he returned most of it to his daughter. This became her dowry, which her husband could never access. It was her security in case her husband died. Effectively, her father gave her *an endowment* so that she might enter her new life with adequate security to face the uncertainties of that life.[433] Thus, her security originated in the sacrifice of her husband and culminated in the generosity of her father.

The Marriage Contract

In Jewish thought, all covenantal relationships were extremely serious. Often, only when they were sealed in blood did they become final and legally binding. The actual terms of the marriage covenant "were spelled out in a formal document called a *ketubah* . . . which stated the bride price . . . the promises and obligations of the groom and listed the rights of the bride. It signified a permanent covenant and an exclusive agreement."[434] The wording of an ancient *ketubah* might be representative:

1. "I will provide you with food, clothing and necessities.
2. "I will redeem you if you are ever taken captive.
3. "I will live with you as a husband according to the universal custom."

Notice that the marriage contract was weighted in the bride's favor. The groom listed "what he would do for *her*, what he would give *her*, and how he would care and provide for *her*."[435] While it is true that we agree "to take upon us the name of [the] Son, and always remember him and keep his commandments,"[436] it is also true that we sometimes forget how much the new and everlasting covenant is weighted in our favor. If we "receive" Jesus, we also receive all that Jesus inherits from his Father, particularly "[the] Father's kingdom . . . [and] all that my Father hath shall be given unto him."[437] "They are they into whose hands the Father has given all things."[438]

The marriage covenant in ancient times was meant to be one of love, security, and comforting assurance. The bridegroom listed promises to always take care of his wife with food, clothing, necessities, redemption, and affectionate attention.[439] We would expect the same treatment from our relationship with the Lord in the Covenant. The text of Psalm 37 in the Jewish *Tanakh* reads: "The Lord is concerned for the needs of the

---

431   Genesis 29:20.
432   Acts 20:28.
433   Nielsen, *Beloved Bridegroom*, 23.
434   Nielsen, *Beloved Bridegroom*, 26, 111.
435   Nielsen, *Beloved Bridegroom*, 111.
436   D&C 20:77.
437   D&C 84:38.
438   D&C 76:55.
439   Nielsen, *Beloved Bridegroom*, 111.

blameless [in this case, the bride]; their portion lasts forever; they shall not come to grief in bad times; in famine, they shall eat their fill. . . . I have never seen a righteous man abandoned, or his children seeking bread. [The Lord] is always generous."[440] By taking some license, we might personalize the promise of continuous caring that Jesus gave to his Apostles on both continents:

> And why take ye thought for raiment? Consider the lilies of the field how they grow; they toil not, neither do they spin; and yet I say unto you, that even Solomon, in all his glory, was not arrayed like one of these. Wherefore, if God so clothe the grass of the field, which today is, and tomorrow is cast into the oven, even so will he clothe you, if ye are not of little faith.
>
> Therefore take no thought, saying, What shall we eat? or, What shall we drink? or, Wherewithal shall we be clothed? For your heavenly Father knoweth that ye have need of all these things. But seek ye first the kingdom of God and his righteousness, and all these things shall be added unto you.[441]

Another stipulation of the marriage contract was the bridegroom's vow to redeem his wife should she ever be taken captive.[442] Lehi assured his son Jacob of the surety of the Lord's redemption: "Wherefore, redemption cometh in and through the Holy Messiah; for he is full of grace and truth. Behold, he offereth himself a sacrifice."[443] All of us have sinned and to one extent or another have been taken captive by the enemy of our souls. Each of us is in need of the Bridegroom's promise of redemption: "and he will take upon him death, that he may loose the bands of death which bind his people."[444] We are reminded of Abraham, a type of the Savior, who assembled an army to rescue Lot and his household from their enemies when they had been taken captive. "And [Abraham] brought back all the goods, and also brought again his brother Lot, and his goods, and the women also, and the people."[445] Thus, by covenant the Bridegroom places all that he has and is, including his own life, on the altar of sacrifice to redeem us from our enemies and to clear every obstacle that stands between us and exaltation.

Finally, the bridegroom anciently promised to live with his wife with love and affection. Donna Nielsen wrote: "The third and last promise in the [marriage contract] was the groom's promise to live as a husband with the bride and to give her an opportunity to bear children. In Hebrew 'to bear children' was synonymous with the term 'to bear fruit.'

---

440 *Tanakh,* Psalms 37:18–19, 25–26.
441 3 Nephi 13:28–33.
442 Nielsen, *Beloved Bridegroom,* 112.
443 2 Nephi 2:6–7.
444 Alma 7:12.
445 Genesis 14:16.

Children were called the 'fruit of the womb' (Luke 1:42)."[446] To first be married (*oneness*) and to then bear fruit (*fruitfulness*) was considered by the ancients to be the measure of one's creation.[447] The *oneness* and *fruitfulness* shared by a husband and wife, and compared to our relationship with the Lord, is described by the Savior (the True Vine) in the following verse: "I am the vine, ye are the branches: He that abideth in me, and I in him, the same bringeth forth much fruit: for without me ye can do nothing."[448] As long as we abide in the Covenant with him, he promises to abide in us, and together our union will be one of abundant fruitfulness.

Moreover, he promises his continuous affection. Nephi called these acts of affection "tender mercies," gentle reminders of his love and awareness; we might consider them "love notes" from the one who knows and adores us most. "Behold, I, Nephi, will show unto you that the tender mercies of the Lord are over all those whom he hath chosen."[449] These evidences of love flow to us quietly but continually; there are a "multitude of his tender mercies."[450] When the bride recognizes her husband's constant goodness, she is brought to tears for her good fortune, just as the Jaredites did upon recognizing the Lord's protection on their journey: "And when they had set their feet upon the shores of the promised land they bowed themselves down upon the face of the land, and did humble themselves before the Lord, and did shed tears of joy before the Lord, because of the multitude of his tender mercies over them."[451]

The marriage contract itself was often elaborately decorated, becoming a piece of art and thus a thing of beauty. It contained the words of a binding and holy agreement, and the bride cherished it. The marriage contract was tangible proof of her future husband's devotion and her immutable rights.[452] In this we again hear overtones of the new and everlasting covenant. No doctrine is more glorious. We cling to the Covenant because it offers us the Bridegroom's guarantees that he will continually provide for us, keep us safe, redeem us from our enemies, and live with us in loving and fruitful companionship. The Covenant promises us the Bridegroom's name, and it reminds us of the great price that he paid for us. The Covenant guarantees that he will endow us with all that he is and has. It states that we, his bride, are his "great treasure," and the Covenant reminds us that he has given his own blood to seal the covenant. What bride would not cherish such a document, especially if it was backed up by years of verifiable devotion?

The Gift of Value

The presentation of the marriage contract was followed by the bridegroom offering his beloved "a token," that is, "a gift of value." This gift was different from the bride price, which the bridegroom had paid to the young woman's father. In this case, the groom offered the

---

446 Nielsen, *Beloved Bridegroom*, 114.
447 Smith, *Restoration of All Things*, 244.
448 John 15:5.
449 1 Nephi 1:20.
450 1 Nephi 8:8.
451 Ether 6:12.
452 Nielsen, *Beloved Bridegroom*, 28.

token directly to his intended bride. "The groom's gift was considered to be an extension of himself.... It also symbolized his willingness to sacrifice and served as a reminder of his love. A gold ring was frequently used as this token or gift because it represented eternity. Anciently, the ring used was often a link from a gold chain. The chain represented past and future family associations and was seen as symbolically linking the girl to her new family."[453]

Sometimes the "gift of value" was silver or gold coins. A devoted bride would often make a chain of the coins and attach them "to her veil as an important part of her headdress." In private and in public, she was spoken for, beloved, and ever abiding in the covenant.[454] If she lost something this valuable, she would view it as a tragedy. Jesus' parable of the lost coin makes more sense in this light; the loss of something so precious could indicate that she had been careless with the token that her betrothed husband had given her. Clearly, our treatment of the Lord's gifts is an indication of our respect for him and the Covenant that we have entered into. The tokens he gives us are the emblems of his sacrifice,[455] represented by the emblems of the sacrament.

The Pledge

After the bridegroom had paid the bride price, offered his beloved the covenantal marriage contract, and given her the token or gift of value, he "recited a ritual statement to consecrate himself to his bride."[456] For example, the biblical prophet, Hosea, speaking for the Lord, pledged, "And I will betroth thee unto me for ever; yea, I will betroth thee unto me in righteousness, and in judgment, and in lovingkindness, and in mercies. I will even betroth thee unto me in faithfulness: and thou shalt know the Lord."[457]

Donna Nielsen explained that the word "consecrate, wherein the groom consecrated himself to the bride, is used to mean, 'to devote irrevocably.' The groom has no options here—no escape clauses—there is no question ever that he would rescind his invitation to the woman to marry. He cannot break this [covenant] if the woman remains faithful, for he is bound if she fulfills her part of the covenant."[458]

Just so, Christ consecrates and devotes himself to us irrevocably when he offers us the Covenant. He will absolutely live up to every promise made in the Covenant. The scriptures are replete with such language. For example: "What I the Lord have spoken, I have spoken, and I excuse not myself; and though the heavens and the earth pass away, my word shall not pass away, but shall all be fulfilled."[459] "Ye know in all your hearts and in all your souls, that not one thing hath failed of all the good things which the Lord your God spake concerning you; all are come to pass unto you, and not one thing hath failed thereof."[460] "Who am I, saith the Lord, that have promised and have not fulfilled?"[461]

---

453 Nielsen, *Beloved Bridegroom*, 28.
454 D&C 98:14; 132:19.
455 "A Poor Wayfaring Man of Grief," *Hymns*, no. 153, verse 7.
456 Nielsen, *Beloved Bridegroom*, 29.
457 Hosea 2:19–20.
458 Nielsen, *Beloved Bridegroom*, 31.
459 D&C 1:38.
460 Joshua 23:14.
461 D&C 58:31.

The Cup to Seal the Covenant

Now the bride had before her the marriage covenant, which stated the bride price, and the token or gift of value. She had heard the bridegroom make an irrevocable pledge stating his eternal devotion and indivisible consecration to her. At this point, he placed before her a cup of wine, which represented blood. Donna Nielsen wrote: "The idea was that the *blood* of the covenant superseded all other loyalties." The wine also signified sacrifice and joy. "These three elements [blood, sacrifice, and joy] were intrinsic to the marriage relationship. . . .

"Now came the suspenseful part. At this point, the woman had about thirty seconds to make up her mind. . . . If the woman was willing to receive the man and his proposed condition, she would accept his gift [token] and also drink the cup of wine, which sealed the covenant. This showed that she was willing to take his name upon her."

When the Savior offers us the new and everlasting covenant, we must not vacillate but rather make a firm decision. Our being "lukewarm" only summons the Savior's rebuke.[462] Elijah became indignant with such indecision: "How long halt ye between two opinions? if the Lord be God, follow him: but if Baal, then follow him."[463] However, in the act of the ancient bride's acceptance, we see glimpses of our saying yes to baptism, receiving the sacrament, and consenting to making our temple covenants and ordinances. Drinking of the marriage cup is implied in every covenant-making instance: "But Jesus answered and said, . . . Are ye able to drink of the cup that I shall drink of, and to be baptized with the baptism that I am baptized with? They say unto him, We are able. And he saith unto them, Ye shall drink indeed of my cup, and be baptized with the baptism that I am baptized with."[464]

The bride's drinking of the cup of wine had to be witnessed by two observers. If and when the bride drank of the cup, the couple was considered betrothed for marriage. "Following the woman's acceptance, the groom, and sometimes the girl's father, recited additional formal statements. . . . To the bride, the groom would speak the words, 'Thou art *set apart* (or consecrated) for me according to the law of Moses and Israel.' Interestingly, the same word for 'set apart,' in the New Testament Greek, '*hagiazo*,' was also used to describe the state of a temple once it was dedicated."[465] The bride's body was now considered a *temple* for her husband. Likewise, when we enter the Covenant, our bodies become temples for the Spirit of the Lord. That idea was suggested by Paul: "Know ye not that your body is the temple of the Holy Ghost which is in you, which ye have of God, and ye are not your own?"[466] "The temple of God is holy, which temple ye are."[467]

All of this suggests, of course, that the marriage covenant represented more than mere ritual or the rehearsing of words. To become valid and eternal, those outward ritualistic actions had to become an inward condition of two hearts bound together by love: "But this shall be the covenant that I will make with the house of Israel [the bride]; after

---

462   Revelation 3:15–16.
463   1 Kings 18:21.
464   Matthew 20:22–23.
465   Nielsen, *Beloved Bridegroom*, 30–31.
466   1 Corinthians 6:19.
467   1 Corinthians 3:17.

those days, saith the Lord, I will put my law in their inward parts, and write it in their hearts; and will be their God, and they shall be my people [my bride]. And they shall teach no more every man his neighbour, and every man his brother, saying, Know the Lord: for they shall all know me, from the least of them unto the greatest of them, saith the Lord."[468] Most intimately and most completely, we will *know* the Bridegroom, and our love would not permit us to violate our Covenant with him. "This is eternal lives—to know the only wise and true God, and Jesus Christ, whom he hath sent. I am he. Receive ye, therefore, my law."[469]

The Covenantal Feast

The betrothal ceremony often ended with a feast at the home of the bride. Included in the feast would be the "breaking of bread." By partaking of the "same loaf at the same table," the participants became bound together as companions. Significantly, the sharing of a meal together *followed* the couple's entering into a covenant.[470]

We cast our thoughts immediately upon the sacrament table and the Lord's supper,[471] which, among other things, reminds us of our previously having entered into the new and everlasting covenant with the Lord through baptism. Additionally, the sacrament reminds us that we are "in waiting," anticipating the time when the Bridegroom will come for us and take us into the place that he has prepared for us in the mansions of his Father.[472] We are always in a state of remembrance, obediently preparing and patiently anticipating the Bridegroom.

The sacrament also helps us to hearken back to the day when we accepted the Lord's proposal and made mutual vows to each other in the presence of two witnesses. That was the day when we formalized our covenant with Lord by being immersed in the living waters of baptism, or, in other words, by drinking fully from the cup of his love.[473] To commemorate the day we entered into the new and everlasting covenant, we eat a covenantal meal containing broken bread from the same loaf. Therefore, by the bread and the cup of wine, we keep in the forefront of our minds our love for and hope in our loving Bridegroom; we hold in sacred remembrance our immutable vows to each other; and we know that he will someday come at an unannounced hour to carry us away to the place that he has prepared for us, our eternal inheritance—our "mansion"—where we will live with him forever in the house of his Father.

The Father's Announcement

Immediately after the betrothal ceremony, the bridegroom's father made the first of two announcements of the upcoming marriage of his son. This announcement, or calling,

---

468 Jeremiah 31:33–34.
469 D&C 132:24.
470 Nielsen, *Beloved Bridegroom*, 20–21, 32.
471 1 Corinthians 11:20.
472 Enos 1:27; Ether 12:32, 34, 37; D&C 98:18.
473 Matthew 20:22–23; 3 Nephi 18:8–9.

is proffered to close friends, family, and others who were invited to the wedding.[474] The scriptures inform us that "many are called"[475] to the wedding because of their relationship with the Father and the Son. If the invited people accepted the father's invitation, they were duty-bound, by covenant, to honor their commitment; that is, they must agree to come to the wedding when it was eventually announced, regardless of the inconvenience of the hour. Donna Nielsen explained: "The initial acceptance obliged the guest to respond to the summons at the 'hour of the banquet.' Only those who accepted the first invitation would receive the final invitation when the feast was ready."[476]

The Bride's Veil

Maidens who were not yet spoken for would be seen in public with unveiled faces. But once they had entered the betrothal or engagement period—that is, when they had entered the Covenant—they veiled their faces in public. This custom, of course, is reminiscent of temple worship. Once the young woman had accepted her beloved's proposal of marriage, she was considered set apart, consecrated, and holy. Therefore, she wore the veil as an indication that she belonged only to her husband and that no one else had the right to appreciate her beauty except him.

As a symbol of her consecration, the bride would forevermore "wear a veil over her hair whenever she was in public. This would indicate her status as a betrothed woman and signal that she was not available to anyone else. She would wear a veil over her hair for the remainder of her life as a symbol of her devotion and faithfulness to her husband. Properly understood, her veil hid only that which was too precious for the common, careless gaze." This was not a sign of inferiority, but rather of glory. Her beauty was to be "enjoyed exclusively by her groom. In fact, only those things which were treasured and glorious were veiled."[477]

Sometimes in scripture Christ becomes the bride instead of the bridegroom, who beckons us to receive *him*. He also symbolically becomes the "veil,"[478] as indicated by the author of Hebrews. This term *veil* seems to signify that we go through him to return to the Father. In this light, other scriptures connecting Christ and the veil begin to take on added meaning. For example, "Sanctify yourselves that your minds become single to God, and the days will come that you will see him; *for he will unveil his face unto you,* and it shall be in his own time, and in his own way, and according to his own will."[479] Only the bridegroom was allowed to look upon the bride's beauty that remained hidden behind the veil. Just so, it is our unique honor to part the veil and gaze upon the glory of the Lord: "And again, verily I say unto you that it is your privilege, and a promise I give unto you that have been ordained unto this ministry, that inasmuch as you strip yourselves from jealousies and fears, and humble yourselves before me, for ye are not sufficiently humble, *the veil shall be rent* and you shall see me and know that I am."[480]

---

474 Nielsen, *Beloved Bridegroom*, 40.
475 D&C 121:40; Matthew 22:14.
476 Nielsen, *Beloved Bridegroom*, 41.
477 Nielsen, *Beloved Bridegroom*, 16, 31.
478 Hebrews 10:20.
479 D&C 88:68; emphasis added.
480 D&C 67:10; emphasis added.

Clearly, that which is most holy is hidden behind the veil. We recall that Moses veiled his face after he returned from speaking with the Lord. His face was filled with so much glory that the people could not endure his presence.[481] That same idea of veiling that which is most holy was represented in the tabernacle and later in the temple of Solomon: a first veil concealed the inside of the temple, and a second veil concealed the Holy of Holies.[482] As we have mentioned, in some respects the bride became a temple to her husband; therefore, in symbolism, she wore the veil to indicate that by covenant her beauty and her loyalties belonged exclusively to her husband.

Likewise, by covenant, we "veil ourselves" from the things of the world and allow no unhallowed hand or glance to remove us from Christ as the Bridegroom, to whom we give exclusively the beauty of the temple of our souls. By covenant, we "come unto Christ [the Bridegroom] . . . and deny [ourselves] of all ungodliness," and we love him with all our "might, mind and strength."[483] Symbolically, we hold sacred those things about ourselves that only the Bridegroom might cherish. "Like a temple," wrote Donna Nielsen, "the woman was now 'set apart' for holiness—the greatest holiness of all."[484]

The Friend of the Bridegroom

The bridegroom paid the bride price, offered his beloved the marriage covenant, gave her a token or emblem, consecrated himself to her, and pledged his enduring devotion. Then the bride indicated her agreement to enter into the marriage covenant by drinking the cup of wine in the presence of witnesses. Finally, the two shared a covenantal meal together. Then, at last, the bridegroom left to prepare a place for her in his father's house. The bridegroom and the bride would not have contact with each other again for about a year. Then, on an unspecified night, he would come suddenly for her and whisk her away.

Until then, the friend of the bridegroom, who had been a witness of the couple's covenant, would act "as liaison between the bride-to-be and the groom during the betrothal period. . . . [He would become] the guarantor of the bride's virgin chastity until the consummation took place. . . . [Later he acted as the] governor at the marriage feast, and finally, his last obligation was announcing to the assembled guests that the full marriage was successfully 'completed.'"[485]

In this tradition, we see obvious symbols of the role of the Holy Ghost, who witnesses our initial covenant-making process. Thereafter, as we wait and prepare for the Lord, the Holy Ghost conveys messages between the Bridegroom and us (the bride). Additionally, he prepares us for the coming of the Bridegroom, encourages us to remain faithful, and, ultimately, when we are finally brought to the wedding, the Holy Ghost justifies us to the Bridegroom and bears testimony of our worthiness. Thus, he oversees the entire

---

481   Exodus 34:29–35.
482   Hebrews 9:1–7.
483   Moroni 10:32.
484   Nielsen, *Beloved Bridegroom*, 31.
485   Nielsen, *Beloved Bridegroom*, 19.

proceedings from start to completion, and in the end he declares the covenantal process is finished. Then the Bridegroom's friend hands us over to the Bridegroom, and the friend's job is completed.

Preparing for Each Other

During the preparation period, which often approached one year, the bridegroom and the bride busied themselves with the primary thing on their minds: their coming wedding. As we have mentioned, the young woman was now considered a bride, so she wore a veil over her hair in public as a token of her new status. Whereas she had belonged to her mother and father, she now belonged to her husband; therefore, she set her relationship with her husband above all other relationships. Her new marriage relationship would define her forevermore: "Therefore shall a man leave his father and his mother, and shall cleave unto his wife: and they shall be one flesh."[486]

For the bride to be separated from her beloved for a year was an exercise in long-suffering and patience. As she prepared for her wedding, she wondered when her bridegroom would come for her. Not knowing the day or hour is a theme regarding the Second Coming that is widely rehearsed in scripture. For example: "The hour and the day no man knoweth, neither the angels in heaven, nor shall they know until he comes."[487] Because the bride did not know the time, she had to live her life in constant anticipation and readiness. Her faithfulness is recalled in the parable of the five virgins whose lamps were trimmed and filled with oil when the bridegroom came.[488] Her example also hearkens to the parable of the chosen few, the handful of faithful Saints among the many who were called to the marriage of the king's son. Only those people who proved themselves worthy were actually allowed to attend the wedding.[489]

The Apostle Paul used the imagery of a woman who was about to give birth: "For yourselves know perfectly that the day of the Lord so cometh as a thief in the night. For when they shall say, Peace and safety; then sudden destruction cometh upon them, *as travail upon a woman with child*; and they shall not escape. But ye, brethren, are not in darkness, that that day should overtake you as a thief."[490] Commenting on this image, Elder Bruce R. McConkie wrote:

> Paul's illustration here is perfect. The Second Coming is compared to a woman about to give birth to a child. She does not know the hour or the minute of the child's arrival, but she does know the approximate time. There are signs which precede and presage the promised arrival. And so it is with our Lord's coming. He shall

---
486 Genesis 2:24.
487 D&C 49:7.
488 Matthew 25:1–13; D&C 45:56–59.
489 Matthew 22:1–14.
490 1 Thessalonians 5:2–4; emphasis added.

> come as a thief in the night, unexpectedly and without warning, to the world, to those who are in spiritual darkness, to those who are not enlightened by the power of the Spirit. But his coming shall not overtake the saints as a thief, for they know and understand the signs of the times.[491]

On difficult days, the bride might have even despaired, wondering if her bridegroom would ever come. Likewise, we might become discouraged when the Lord "delays his coming" to our aid. Nevertheless, we are counseled to watch, pray, and not faint while waiting.[492] We are to "seek the face of the Lord always, that in patience ye may possess your souls, and ye shall have eternal life."[493] In every difficulty, the Lord will eventually come for us. Even if the time is protracted, he will come. The Lord told Isaiah, "Say to them that are of a fearful heart, Be strong, fear not: behold, your God will come . . . ; he will come and save you."[494] We are assured that "he remembereth every creature of his creating, he will make himself manifest unto all."[495] "Ye may know of a surety that I, the Lord God, do visit my people in their afflictions."[496] Most certainly, the Bridegroom will come; it is not a matter of *if* but *when*.

To comfort and help the bride endure his absence, the bridegroom left in her possession reminders of his promise to return—"I go away and come again unto you"[497]—which symbolize his enduring love for her. These reminders, which she holds close to her heart, are the bride price, the marriage contract, and the token. When he left her, he knew her wait would be difficult. His pledge is reminiscent of his words to us: "Let not your hearts be troubled; for in my Father's house are many mansions, and I have prepared a place for you; and where my Father and I am, there ye shall be also."[498] And at another time, he said, "I go to prepare a place for you."[499]

It is important here to realize that during the separation period the bridegroom was also preparing for his bride; she was not preparing alone. Additionally, although he would be physically absent from her, he had arranged to provide for her safety and her comfort. He assigned his trusted friend or "comforter" to watch over her until he returned. We recall that when Jesus announced his imminent departure, he said to the Apostles, "I will not leave you comfortless."[500] As we have mentioned, the Lord's "friend" is the Holy Ghost.

During the protracted betrothal period, the bridegroom spent his time building his beloved a bridal chamber within the confines of his father's house or estate. After the wedding, the chamber would become their home. Donna Nielsen explained, "The

---

491 McConkie, *Doctrinal New Testament Commentary*, 3:54.
492 Matthew 26:41; Luke 1:18.
493 D&C 101:38.
494 Isaiah 35:4.
495 Mosiah 27:30.
496 Mosiah 24:14.
497 John 14:28.
498 D&C 98:18.
499 John 14:2.
500 John 14:18.

new home was built under the direct personal supervision of the groom's father. In that culture, a son is considered to be a representative of his father, and everything that the son does reflects either favorably or unfavorably on the father. . . . With such close identification between a father and his son, the father wanted everything regarding the bride's new home to be as beautiful and perfect as it could be. . . . The father of the groom was the sole judge of when the preparations were complete. . . . When the father determined everything was ready, he gave permission for the son to claim his bride. No one knew when that permission was forthcoming; . . . only the father knew."[501] The bride would not see her bridegroom until the night he came for her, which time was hidden from her. Thus, the bride spent the betrothal period preparing for the time that her bridegroom, who was also preparing, would finally receive his father's commission, and suddenly appear with little warning to whisk her away to the "mansion" that he had prepared for her.

The Serious Nature of Preparing

The subjects of preparing for the Bridegroom's return and receiving an inheritance in his Father's kingdom occupy chapter 25 of Matthew. This chapter describes who and what we are preparing for, how we must prepare, and how the principle of stewardship assists us to prepare. Here the Lord gives three parables—the parable of the ten virgins, the parable of the talents, and the parable of the sheep and the goats. Kent P. Jackson wrote:

> These allegories seem to form a progression, teaching different aspects of readiness that Jesus encouraged of His listeners and readers. The Joseph Smith translation of verse 1 places the story of the ten virgins clearly in the context of the Second Coming. . . . (Matthew 25:1–13.) Preparation is a necessary precaution because "ye know neither the day nor the hour wherein the Son of Man cometh." This parable . . . ends with the admonition, "Watch!"
>
> In the parable of the Talents (Matthew 25:14–30), the master, traveling to "a far country," leaves different quantities of his goods in the hands of three servants, to each "according to his several ability." Two of the servants doubled their master's resources that had been entrusted to them. The third, however, hid his allotment for safekeeping. To the two who magnified their investment, the master said upon his return, "Well done, good and faithful servant; thou hast been faithful over a few things, I will make thee ruler over

---

501   Nielsen, *Beloved Bridegroom*, 34–35.

many things: enter thou into the joy of thy lord." The final servant returned the master's talent to him, yet he did not receive his lord's praise but rather his condemnation: "Thou wicked and slothful servant." This is not a parable about the uncertain timing of Christ's return but about what we are to do with the gifts He has entrusted to us while we were waiting. As Joseph Smith taught, we should "improve upon all things committed to [our] charge." This parable . . . ends with the unprofitable servant's intense sorrow, "weeping and gnashing of teeth."

The final parable, that of the Sheep and the Goats (see Matthew 25:31–46), again addresses what people do with the blessings entrusted to them—but in a different way. The setting . . . is a judgment scene: "When the Son of Man shall come in his glory . . . and he shall separate them one from another, as a shepherd divideth his sheep from the goats." Those placed on his right hand will receive an inheritance in His kingdom, whereas those on his left hand will be sent off to "everlasting fire." Jesus explained in some detail the criteria for the King's just judgment. Those worthy of an inheritance of glory will be those who fed Him when he was hungry, gave Him drink when he was thirsty, took Him in when He was a stranger, clothed Him when He was naked, visited Him when He was sick, and came to Him when He was in prison. Those who will be condemned will be the ones who had the same opportunities but did none of those worthy things.[502]

The burden of stewardship is intrinsically linked to our preparation for the Lord's Second Coming. In this context, we are both the bride and the steward. First, as the bride, we must anticipate the Bridegroom's arrival in an attitude of constant readiness, as a betrothed bride would prepare and watch as she waited for the promised return of her beloved. She would "always remember him."[503] Just so, during our wait, we are to remain absolutely loyal to the Bridegroom. We are not to divide our affections with another. Our entire attention is to prepare for the coming wedding when we will be *more surely* joined with the Bridegroom and live with him forevermore. Again, the one who helps us to prepare and who comforts us so that we can endure the wait is the Bridegroom's "friend," the Holy Ghost. We are also comforted by holding in our possession the price that the

---

[502] Jackson, "The Olivet Discourse," in Holzapfel and Wayment, *From the Transfiguration through the Triumphant Entry*, 342–43.
[503] D&C 20:77.

Bridegroom paid for us, the Covenant he made with us, and the tokens (his wounds, as symbolized in the sacrament) that he gave to us.

In our dual roles of bride and steward, we receive from the Lord both gifts and stewardships to help us endure the wait and to prepare: (1) as the "bride," we receive from the Lord gifts to help us remember him and his promise to return; (2) as the "steward," we receive from the Lord stewardships as sacred trusts to manage his property (that which he has given us and those callings he has extended to us) and resources (time, talents, spiritual gifts, etc.) until he returns. As both the bride and the steward, we are to anticipate the Lord's return and actively prepare for it. As the steward, we are to magnify our stewardships during the wait. We do so by using the resources and surpluses of our stewardships to bless the Lord's children. As the steward and the bride, we have covenanted to take upon us his name, and therefore we belong to him. As his bride, his children become our children, and we share in his efforts to take care of them.

Both the loyal bride and the faithful steward are "accounted worthy to inherit the mansions prepared for him of my Father."[504] But, as both the bride and the steward, if we do not prepare for the Bridegroom, if we do not remain loyal to him, if we do not listen to his Friend, if we are ashamed of the gifts he has given us or hide or misuse our stewardships or do not use them as he has instructed (to bless the lives of others)—if we do any of these things, he will say to us when he comes that he does not know us: "Depart from me." Then, sadly, we will have forfeited the marriage. In that miserable state, we will be cast away to where there is "weeping and gnashing of teeth." We will find ourselves on the Lord's left hand, the place that is called "cursed" and described as "everlasting fire prepared for the devil and his angels."[505]

Clearly, the Bridegroom expects his bride to hold his name in high regard, to always remember him, and to remain loyal to their marriage covenant. To the extent that the bride remains faithful, she will have the Bridegroom's Friend to attend, comfort, instruct, and prepare her for the Bridegroom's coming and for the wedding.

The Bride's Final Preparations

As we have mentioned, the ancient Jewish bride did not know the exact day and hour of the bridegroom's coming, but her relationship with the bridegroom's friend would have provided her with signs of the bridegroom's coming. As the approximate time approached, she intensified her preparations. She kept herself adorned. She practiced applying wedding makeup, and she paid special attention to her fingernails, hair, and skin so that she would appear as attractive as possible for her new husband. Also, from the time of the bridegroom's departure, and she kept a lamp burning brightly in her window until he came for her.[506]

"As the time of the wedding drew closer, the young girl anxiously awaited her groom's arrival. By custom, it would be sudden, with an element of surprise, and often

---

504 D&C 72:3–4.
505 Matthew 25:12, 30, 41.
506 Nielsen, *Beloved Bridegroom*, 36, 38.

late at night. She invited her sisters, cousins, and friends to join her vigil and be supportive at this time of joyous anticipation. . . . Night after night, they would strain to hear the shouts of the bridegroom and his friends."[507]

This custom is illustrated, of course, in Jesus' parable of the ten virgins. We recall that the vigil had gone on a long time and that the bridegroom had "tarried." Then, "at midnight there was a cry made, Behold, the bridegroom cometh; go ye out to meet him."[508] Intrinsic in the new and everlasting covenant is the stipulation that we, the bride, "watch." That is, we must live in a state of happy anticipation and preparation, "for ye know neither the day nor the hour wherein the Son of man cometh."[509]

In the last days before her wedding, the bride would submit to a ritual washing and anointing because she was about to become royalty. At her wedding, according to the custom, she would become a queen and would be presented to a king.[510] In a special pool called a *mikvah*, the bride immersed herself completely in "living waters." "Her life and her body were to be the gift of a living sacrifice to her husband, and to be pure without spot or blemish was a condition required of sacrifices (Ephesians 5:27; Romans 12:1). . . . The Jewish bride did not immerse herself because of uncleanness, but in preparation for holiness, to fulfill God's commandment to be fruitful and multiply. . . . After her immersion in the *mikvah*, the bride's friends would help her anoint herself as part of the preparation for marriage."[511] This ceremonial immersion in living water symbolized, among other things, "a preparation for holiness." Additionally, "it also represented a separation from an old life to a new life—from life as a single woman to life as a married woman."[512]

As part of the new and everlasting covenant, we are also to go into a holy place (the temple) "to prepare . . . for the ordinances and endowments, washings and anointing."[513] The visual image of washing relates to the process of purification that eliminates impurities, contaminants, and pollutants.[514] We are washed, or purified, in preparation to be anointed and thus sanctified. The idea of anointing[515] speaks to the process of changing the purpose of something or someone.[516] By ceremonially washing and anointing her body, the bride avowed that she was clean and ready for her life's purpose to change; she was now ready to be endowed with the fulness of the marriage covenant and thus become a queen in Israel. By the rituals of washing (purification) and anointing (sanctification), the bride demonstrated her willingness to become totally consecrated to her husband and yield to the transformation of her life's purpose. Now all was in order for her to join with her husband, who would be her king.[517]

---

507 Nielsen, *Beloved Bridegroom*, 39.
508 Matthew 25:5–6.
509 Matthew 25:13.
510 Nielsen, *Beloved Bridegroom*, 38.
511 Nielsen, *Beloved Bridegroom*, 37–38.
512 Nielsen, *Beloved Bridegroom*, 125.
513 Smith, *Teachings of the Prophet Joseph Smith*, 308.
514 Isaiah 4:4; Psalm 51:2.
515 Leviticus 8:10–12.
516 D&C 20:77.
517 Nielsen, *Beloved Bridegroom*, 44.

Interestingly, the bridegroom, although it was not required, usually also submitted himself to a washing in the *mikvah* to purify himself in preparation for the wedding. This voluntary washing reminds us that the Savior submitted to baptism although he was sinless. His purpose in receiving the ordinance was to enter the new and everlasting covenant and "fulfil all righteousness."[518] Later, at the end of his life, he also voluntarily sanctified himself so that he might better help others to become sanctified so that they could become *one* with him: "And for their sakes I sanctify myself, that they also might be sanctified through the truth. . . . That they all may be one; as thou, Father, art in me, and I in thee, that they also may be one in us."[519] Thus we see Jesus submitting to the processes of purification and sanctification to prepare himself to become *one* with those whom he loved. It is said that Jesus Christ is our *Mikvah-Israel,* which means "hope of Israel."[520]

Invitation to the Wedding

When the bridegroom completed the "little mansion or bridal chamber"[521] for his bride, and when the groom's father finally declared that the construction and preparations met his approval, the father at last gave his son permission to go and claim his bride. Immediately, the bridegroom began to organize a wedding procession by calling and gathering his close associates. In this we remember the reference to the Lord's coming with "all the holy angels with him."[522]

While the bridegroom was thus engaged, the father sent his servants to make the second announcement or, in other words, "for the last time."[523] We recall that the first announcement, or calling, happened at the time of betrothal. At that time, the invited guests covenanted to come to the wedding whenever the father announced that the wedding, feast, and festivities were about to commence.[524] We must keep in mind that the chosen ones had promised that they would remain in readiness and attend the marriage of the son. To reject the invitation now would be nothing short of a monumental insult and a serious offense. Jesus spoke about the second "announcement" and the seriousness of following through on our initial covenant:

> A certain man made a great supper, and bade many:
> And sent his servant at supper time to say to them that were bidden, Come; for all things are now ready.
> And they all with one consent began to make excuse. The first said unto him, I have bought a piece of ground, and I must needs go and see it: I pray thee have me excused.

---

518 Matthew 3:15.
519 John 17:19, 21.
520 Nielsen, *Beloved Bridegroom,* 125, quoting a rabbi from the first century.
521 Nielsen, *Beloved Bridegroom,* 33.
522 Matthew 25:31.
523 Jacob 5:62–64; D&C 24:19; 39:17; 43:28; 88:84; 95:4; 112:30.
524 Nielsen, *Beloved Bridegroom,* 40.

> And another said, I have bought five yoke of oxen, and I go to prove them: I pray thee have me excused.
>
> And another said, I have married a wife, and therefore I cannot come.
>
> So that servant came, and shewed his lord these things. Then the master of the house being angry said to his servant, Go out quickly into the streets and lanes of the city, and bring in hither the poor, and the maimed, and the halt, and the blind.
>
> And the servant said, Lord, it is done as thou hast commanded, and yet there is room.
>
> And the lord said unto the servant, Go out into the highways and hedges, and compel them to come in, that my house may be filled.
>
> For I say unto you, That none of those men which were bidden shall taste of my supper.[525]

Notice that the chosen guests who did not attend the wedding used as excuses property, possessions, and family concerns. It is sad but true that many of the chosen ones will step aside from their covenant: "Behold, there are many called, but few are chosen. And why are they not chosen? Because their hearts are set so much upon the things of this world, and aspire to the honors of men."[526] For an invited guest to place anything above his commitment to attend the wedding, or for an invited guest to be unprepared, as were five of the ten virgins, is an insult that will summon the Father's indignation. Not responding to the Bridegroom's invitation at his advent will most certainly result in such individuals being shut out from the wedding and the Bridegroom denying that he knows them.[527]

The Wedding Processional

In ancient Jewish practice, the bridegroom led a procession to the bride's home to claim her. He was arrayed in regal attire, often wearing a crown, dressed in garments "scented with frankincense and myrrh," and appearing in every way like a king. This joyous occasion was one of "singing, dancing and merriment." Now the bridegroom's long-awaited purpose and object of his sacrifice were about to be realized.[528] The clamorous late-night procession wound through the streets with its torches beaming and trumpets blaring, awakening everyone along the way. The scriptures inform us that "the Son of Man shall come, and he shall send his angels before him with the great sound of a trumpet." Those in the procession beckoned others to join them, as the Savior will: "And they shall gather together the remainder of his elect from the four winds, from one end of heaven to the other."[529]

---

525 Luke 14:16–24.
526 D&C 121:34–35.
527 Matthew 25:1–13.
528 Nielsen, *Beloved Bridegroom*, 41.
529 JS–Matthew 1:37.

When the procession neared the bride's home, "a messenger was sent ahead to give the shout, 'The bridegroom cometh!'" At that point, the bride had about half an hour "to make final preparations" before the shout was given again and the bridegroom arrived.[530] So shall it be at the Savior's Second Coming: "And he [the angelic messenger] shall sound his trump both long and loud, and all nations shall hear it. *And there shall be silence in heaven for the space of half an hour*; and immediately after shall the curtain of heaven be unfolded, as a scroll is unfolded after it is rolled up, and the face of the Lord shall be unveiled."[531]

Claiming the Bride

Ancient Jewish marriage is filled with the imagery of the new and everlasting covenant. Part of the marriage ceremony consists of the groom coming to claim his bride, much as Christ has and will claim us through the power of his Atonement. When we enter into the Covenant with the Bridegroom through baptism, we recognize the fact that he has paid a price for us. In the covenantal agreement, he promises to provide for us, redeem us, and to live with us in a loving relationship. Then he presents us with tokens (his wounds) representing his love and devotion. He does all of this in the presence of witnesses. He vows to prepare a place for us in the mansions of his Father, and he promises to one day return for us: "I will come again, and receive you unto myself; that where I am, there ye may be also."[532] When at last he finally comes to claim us, we, together, will make the marriage complete and he will *seal us his*.[533]

The hour had finally come for the loyal and long-suffering bride. Having made all proper preparations, having waited faithfully and patiently for the bridegroom's return, having heard the trumpet and the shout, having gathered everything together during the last half hour, and having heard the final shout, the bride now gave herself willingly to the bridegroom as he burst through the door of her home to claim her. By this action, the bridegroom suddenly elevated his bride to the stature of a queen.

The new and everlasting covenant provides for such regal unity: "[The Bridegroom] hast made us unto our God kings and priests [and queens and priestesses]: and we shall reign on the earth."[534] Elder Bruce R. McConkie wrote: "This unity among all the saints, and between them and the Father and the Son, is reserved for those who gain exaltation and inherit the fulness of the Father's kingdom. Those who attain it will all know the same things; think the same thoughts; exercise the same powers; do the same acts; respond in the same way to the same circumstances; beget the same kind of offspring; rejoice in the same continuation of the seeds forever; create the same type of worlds; enjoy the same eternal fulness; and glory in the same exaltation."[535]

Immediately, the bride was lifted up into a special chair—a throne—"and carried to her new home. . . . four strong men" who conveyed the bride were "given the honor-

---

530 Nielsen, *Beloved Bridegroom*, 42.
531 D&C 88:94–95; emphasis added.
532 John 14:2–3.
533 Mosiah 5:15.
534 Revelation 5:10.
535 McConkie, *Mormon Doctrine*, 814.

ary title, *Giborei Yisrael,* or heroes of Israel."[536] In this regal setting, the bride appeared stunningly beautiful, without spot or blemish. Moreover, she was beautiful within, having prepared and faithfully endured during the wait. Similarly, the Apostle John saw latter-day Zion "prepared as a bride adorned for her husband."[537] The psalmist wrote, "The king's daughter is all glorious within: her clothing is of wrought gold. She shall be brought unto the king in raiment of needlework: the virgins her companions that follow her shall be brought unto thee. With gladness and rejoicing shall they be brought: they shall enter into the king's palace."[538]

Now the bridegroom brought her to the place he had prepared for her. Donna Nielsen explained: "The most important period of the marriage festivities was when the bride entered her new home. The bride and groom were sometimes crowned with real crowns or with garlands or roses, myrtle, or olive leaves. . . . The couple was treated like royalty during this time. The new husband was literally considered a king and priest in his own home, with his wife as queen."[539] How glorious is the Covenant that exalts us and makes us one with the King of Heaven!

The Wedding

A number of symbolic events occurred when the guests entered into the father's home. These events point to blessings that attend the new and everlasting covenant. For example, each guest had his feet and hands washed; then he was anointed, embraced, and kissed. These gestures were evidences of reconciliation; no hard feelings would be allowed in the father's house on such a joyous occasion. We might expect to be thus treated when we regain the Father's presence.

"Another Jewish custom was to wear a 'wedding garment.'" These garments were supplied to the guests by the bridegroom's father. They were white, "a color associated with royalty." Moreover, the white garments represented light. If someone were found not wearing a garment, such as the guest mentioned in Matthew 22:11, his action would be interpreted as disdain for the father's generosity, and he would be cast out.

While the guests were dressing, greeting, and conversing, the bridegroom and the bride dressed in their white wedding clothing, which was symbolic of "purity, forgiveness of sins, and solemn joy."[540] Isaiah exulted, "I will greatly rejoice in the Lord, my soul shall be joyful in my God; for he hath clothed me with the garments of salvation, he hath covered me with the robe of righteousness, as a bridegroom decketh himself with ornaments, and as a bride adorneth herself with her jewels."[541]

At this point, the bride would be anointed with sweet olive oil. We remember that this sanctifying act signified her joy and her willingness to transform her life as a single woman to a life as queen to her husband. This change of status was shared by both the

---

536 Nielsen, *Beloved Bridegroom,* 43.
537 Revelation 21:2.
538 Psalms 45:13–15.
539 Nielsen, *Beloved Bridegroom,* 44.
540 Nielsen, *Beloved Bridegroom,* 51–54.
541 Isaiah 61:10.

bride and the bridegroom. "Each groom at the time of his wedding and later in his own home was to be considered as a king and a priest." The act of clothing the couple in royal wedding robes signified, among other things, that they were now consecrated to become fruitful and bear children.[542] Similarly, the Covenant, like royal robes, wraps us in "the bond of charity, as with a mantle, which is the bond of perfectness and peace."[543] Then, like the purposes of the bridegroom and his beloved change from profane to holy by the act of marriage, and now they are capable of being fruitful, so we, when we are joined with the Lord, the True Vine, in the Covenant, experience a mighty change of purpose and become fruitful in him.[544]

Now the time of the wedding was at hand. The place of making the covenant was under a canopy, a square piece of cloth held up by four poles. The canopy was open on all sides, reminiscent of the hospitality Abraham and Sarah showed guests in their open tent. The canopy was usually positioned outside so as to be under the stars. Symbolically, it represented, among other things, "God's sheltering love," and also the covenant that God made with Abraham, promising that his children would be as numerous as the stars of the heavens.[545] Likewise, when we marry in the temple, we are sealed together in the presence of the luminaries of heaven and blessed with all the blessings of Abraham, including "a fulness and a continuation of the seeds forever and ever."[546]

After the bridegroom had been escorted to the canopy by his parents, the bride was brought to the canopy by hers. At that point, the "officiator faced the couple and read the Psalm of Thanksgiving (Psalm 100). A goblet of wine was raised, and a blessing was said over the wine. This was called the 'Cup of Joy.' Both the bride and the bridegroom drank from the same cup, indicating they would share the joys of life together." Likewise, we are yoked to Jesus in the new and everlasting covenant.[547] Our Bridegroom has covenanted to share with us all the joys and sorrows of life; by covenant, we will never be left alone.

Then the bridegroom placed a ring, representing eternity, on the bride's right index finger. It was the right hand that was used for making covenants. At that point, the bridegroom "lifted the bride's veil and placed the corner of it on his shoulder. This was a proclamation to everyone present that the government of his bride now rested on his shoulder," an image that Isaiah used to describe the Savior's relationship to us.[548] Then the marriage contract was read aloud for all to witness, followed by the officiator reciting blessings. Similarly, the Lord pronounces blessings upon those whom he seals together:

> And again, verily I say unto you, if a man marry a
> wife by my word, which is my law, and by the new and
> everlasting covenant, and it is sealed unto them by

---

542 Nielsen, *Beloved Bridegroom*, 52, 54–55.
543 D&C 88:125.
544 John 15:5–8.
545 Nielsen, *Beloved Bridegroom*, 55–56.
546 D&C 132:19.
547 Matthew 11:29–30.
548 Isaiah 9:6.

the Holy Spirit of promise, by him who is anointed, unto whom I have appointed this power and the keys of this priesthood; and it shall be said unto them—Ye shall come forth in the first resurrection . . . and shall inherit thrones, kingdoms, principalities, and powers, dominions, all heights and depths . . . , and if ye abide in my covenant, and commit no murder whereby to shed innocent blood, it shall be done unto them in all things whatsoever my servant hath put upon them, in time, and through all eternity; and shall be of full force when they are out of the world; and they shall pass by the angels, and the gods, which are set there, to their exaltation and glory in all things, as hath been sealed upon their heads, which glory shall be a fulness and a continuation of the seeds forever and ever.

Then shall they be gods, because they have no end; therefore shall they be from everlasting to everlasting, because they continue; then shall they be above all, because all things are subject unto them. Then shall they be gods, because they have all power, and the angels are subject unto them.[549]

Next, the officiator offered a second cup of wine to the couple. "This cup was called the 'Cup of Sacrifice' and the 'Cup of Salvation.' They would have to share sacrifices in life, but eventually those sacrifices would be a source of salvation for both of them."[550] Likewise, in the Covenant, the Bridegroom vows to walk the path of life by our side. Against all odds, he drank of the cup of sacrifice for our salvation: "the cup which my Father hath given me, shall I not drink it?"[551] Our life together is one of mutual sacrifice that most assuredly will lead to our salvation. In the Covenant, we counsel and make decisions together; we love together; we hurt together. What he wants, we want. We share our hopes, desires, and dreams, and we also share our sorrows. We are one.

Drinking from the cup of sacrifice or the cup of salvation is vividly described in the Savior's own words: "For behold, I, God, have suffered these things for all, that they might not suffer if they would repent; but if they would not repent they must suffer even as I; which suffering caused myself, even God, the greatest of all, to tremble because of pain, and to bleed at every pore, and to suffer both body and spirit—and would that I might not drink the bitter cup, and shrink—nevertheless, glory be to the Father, and I partook and finished my preparations unto the children of men."[552]

---

549   D&C 132:19–20.
550   Nielsen, *Beloved Bridegroom*, 57–60.
551   John 18:11.
552   D&C 19:16–19.

The Bridegroom's Plea

No doctrine is more glorious than the new and everlasting covenant. Significantly, the Bridegroom initiates the invitation to join with him in a covenantal relationship that is as holy, loving, intimate, fruitful, trusting, and enduring as an eternal marriage. Equally significant is the fact that in inviting us to enter into a covenant relationship, the Lord essentially pleads with us that we will have mercy on *him* that we might agree to join with him. That is, he desires our steadfast love and loyalty above all else. This is an interesting twist considering the fact that we are ever pleading for *his* mercy, love, and loyalty.

We begin to understand this gospel irony when we note that the Hebrew word for mercy is *hesed*, which "refers to the deep spiritual and emotional bond that exists between two very close people such as husband and wife. Immediately, one perceives that God wants us to be as emotionally and spiritually close to him in thought and action as a devoted husband and wife would be. . . . It is a humbling moment when we realize that such a powerful, loving, and kind God wants this type of a relationship. Such knowledge inspires one to 'grow up' spiritually and to think more about the impact his life has on God."[553]

That the Lord would literally plead with us to enter into a covenantal relationship with him evokes tender images. At the end of his earthly ministry, we recall that Jesus lamented over proud Jerusalem, the bride whom he had courted for so long, the bride whom he would have gathered to him so many times in protective and loving care—the bride who would not give him her love.[554] That image evokes the vision of a prospective groom who has loved a woman for a long time and has finally managed to gather enough to pay a substantial bride price by sacrificing his all. Now he hands her a document written on fine parchment which contains his covenantal promises: He will provide for her, redeem her, love her, and give her his name. Then he offers her a token or a gift of value, a representation of his promises, and, in the presence of witnesses, recites a pledge to irrevocably bind and consecrate himself to her forever. He places a cup of wine before her. . . and waits. Will she drink of the cup or will she refuse him?

How we respond to the Bridegroom's invitation will determine our eternal future. A great and potentially divisive decision lies before each of us. Those who neglect or reject the Lord's proposal to enter into the new and everlasting covenant will find themselves on his left hand, symbolically (to the Jewish mind) the hand of disdain. Conversely, those who accept the Lord's proposal and thereafter live faithfully in the Covenant will find themselves on his right hand, the hand of covenant making, the hand on which the bride accepts her husband's ring.[555] Jesus commented on this reality in words of stark imagery:

> When the Son of man shall come in his glory, and all
> the holy angels with him, then shall he sit upon the

---

553 Nielsen, *Beloved Bridegroom*, iv.
554 Matthew 23:37.
555 Nielsen, *Beloved Bridegroom*, 57.

> throne of his glory: And before him shall be gathered all nations: and he shall separate them one from another, as a shepherd divideth [his] sheep from the goats: And he shall set the sheep on his right hand, but the goats on the left.
>
> Then shall the King say unto them on his right hand, Come, ye blessed of my Father, inherit the kingdom prepared for you from the foundation of the world. . . . Then shall he say also unto them on the left hand, Depart from me, ye cursed, into everlasting fire, prepared for the devil and his angels.[556]

May we respond to the Lord's plea and accept his invitation to join him in the new and everlasting covenant. Then we, like the bride, will stand forever on the Bridegroom's right hand and there exult as did Jeremiah: "This is the joy and rejoicing of mine heart: for I am called by thy name, O Lord God of hosts."[557]

Postlude

The first pillar of Zion is the new and everlasting covenant. It stands as the premier covenant that creates a Zion-like life. To formally accept the Atonement of Jesus Christ, we must enter into the new and everlasting covenant by baptism, and then follow the Covenant to its perfect conclusion. The path we will follow is called the *strait and narrow path*, and it is marked with other covenants that we must take upon us.

In review, the new and everlasting covenant consists of two primary covenants: the covenant of baptism and the oath and covenant of the priesthood. The priesthood covenant is magnified by (1) ordination for worthy men; (2) temple covenants and ordinances for worthy men and women; (3) the temple sealing covenant, which is called the covenant of exaltation,[558] for worthy men and women.

In total, these covenants, which emerge from the new and everlasting covenant, cleanse us, separate us from the world, prepare us for coronation, and protect us from Satan. They endow us with keys to the knowledge and power of God, and they establish us in our eternal kingdoms.

The new and everlasting covenant defines the road to becoming a Zion person, and Zion, we have learned, is our ideal and the standard among celestial and celestial-seeking people.[559] If our desire is truly to achieve Zion in our lives, we must enter into this Covenant and make a contract, which is agreed to by each member of the Godhead. Initially, we might perceive the Covenant as a series of laws, but as we spend time in the Covenant, we soon discover that it is a manifestation of love. In a most remarkable way,

---

556   Matthew 25:31–34, 41.
557   Jeremiah 15:16.
558   D&C 105:5.
559   D&C 97:21.

the Covenant is like a marriage covenant, with love as the foundational motivator. Ultimately, we discover that the Covenant is all about our relationship with God. He invites us into a union that he describes in terms of marriage, the most holy, intimate, fruitful, trusting, and enduring of all relationships.

Thus, we end as we began: To become Zion people and thus ensure our salvation and exaltation, we must enter into the new and everlasting covenant and abide in it forevermore. By this, we witness that we have made a choice between Zion and Babylon. Furthermore, we witness that we agree to follow the Covenant to its perfect end: to be snatched from Babylon, to be singled out, to be purified and have our hearts sanctified, to be prepared in every way to regain the presence of God, and to obtain our inheritance and our crown. "This is Zion: THE PURE IN HEART."

Bibliography

American Heritage Dictionary. Boston, MA: Houghton Mifflin, 2000.

Anderson, Dawn Hall, Susette Fletcher Green, and Dlora Hall Dalton, eds. *Clothed with Charity: Talks from the 1996 Women's Conference.* Salt Lake City, UT: Deseret Book, 1997.

Asay, Carlos E. "The Oath and Covenant of the Priesthood," *Ensign,* November 1985.

—*Family Pecan Trees: Planting a Legacy of Faith at Home.* Salt Lake City, UT: Deseret Book, 1992.

—*The Seven M's of Missionary Service: Proclaiming the Gospel as a Member or Full-time Missionary.* Salt Lake City, UT: Bookcraft, 1996.

Ashton, Marvin J. "Be a Quality Person," *Ensign,* February 1993.

—"Love Takes Time," *Ensign,* November 1975.

Bednar, David A. "Pray Always," *Ensign,* November 2008.

Benson, Ezra Taft. "A Vision and a Hope for the Youth of Zion," *Devotional Speeches of the Year.* Provo, UT: Brigham Young University Press, 1978.

—*A Witness and a Warning: A Modern-Day Prophet Testifies of the Book of Mormon.* Salt Lake City, UT: Deseret Book, 1988.

—"Beware of Pride," *Ensign,* May 1989.

—*Devotional Speeches of the Year.* Provo, UT: Brigham Young University Press, 1978.

—*God, Family, Country: Our Three Great Loyalties.* Salt Lake City, UT: Deseret Book, 1975.

—"In His Steps," *Ensign,* September 1988.

—"Jesus Christ—Gifts and Expectations," *New Era,* May 1975.

—*The Teachings of Ezra Taft Benson.* Salt Lake City, UT: Deseret Book, 1988.

—"What I Hope You Will Teach Your Children about the Temple," *Ensign,* August 1985;

Bible Dictionary. Salt Lake City, UT: The Church of Jesus Christ of Latter-day Saints, 1989;

Black, Susan Easton, et al. *Doctrines for Exaltation: The 1989 Sperry Symposium on the Doctrine and Covenants.* Salt Lake City, UT: Deseret Book, *1989.*

—*The Iowa Mormon Trail: Legacy of Faith and Courage.* Orem, UT: Helix Publishing, 1997.

Bowen, Albert E. *The Church Welfare Plan.* Salt Lake City, UT: The Church of Jesus Christ of Latter-day Saints, 1946.

Brewster, Hoyt W. Jr. *Doctrine and Covenants Encyclopedia.* Salt Lake City, UT: Bookcraft, 1988.

Brown, Hugh B. *Continuing the Quest.* Salt Lake City, UT: Bookcraft, 1961.

Brown, Matthew B. *Prophecies: The Gate of Heaven.* American Fork, UT: Covenant Communications, 1999.

—*Signs of the Times, Second Coming, Millenium.* American Fork, UT: Covenant Communications, 2006.

Budge, Ernest A. Wallis. *Coptic Martyrdoms Discourse on Abbaton. London: British Museum,* 1914.

Burton, Alma P., ed. *Discourses of the Prophet Joseph Smith.* Salt Lake City, UT: Deseret Book, 1956.

Cannon, Donald Q. *Teachings of the Latter-day Prophets.* Salt Lake City, UT: Bookcraft, 1998.

Cannon, Elaine. "Agency and Accountability." Salt Lake City, *Ensign,* November 1983.

Bibliography

Cannon, George Q. "Beware Lest Ye Fall." Discourse delivered at the Morgan Utah Stake Conference, Sunday, February 16, 1896.

—*Gospel Truth: Discourses and Writings of President George Q. Cannon.* Salt Lake City, UT: Deseret Book, 1974.

Cannon, Joseph A. "Sanctification," *Mormon Times*, June 12, 2008, http://www.mormontimes.com.

Clark, E. Douglas. *The Blessings of Abraham—Becoming a Zion People.* American Fork, UT: Covenant Communications, 2005.

Clark, J. Reuben. *Church Welfare Plan: A Discussion. Salt Lake, City,* UT General Church Welfare Committee, 1939.

Clark, James R., comp., *Messages of the First Presidency of The Church of Jesus Christ of Latter-day Saints.* Salt Lake City: Bookcraft, 1965–75.

Clarke, Adam. *Clarke's Commentary on the Bible.* Grand Rapids, MI: Baker Book House, 1967.

Clarke, J. Richard. "Successful Welfare Stewardship," *Ensign*, November 1978.

Conference Report, 1897–2009, Salt Lake City, UT: The Church of Jesus Christ of Latter-day Saints.

Cook, Gene R. "Home and Family: A Divine Eternal Pattern," *Ensign*, May 1984.

—"The Seat Next to You," *New Era*, October 1983.

Cook, Lyndon. *Joseph Smith and the Law of Consecration.* Provo, UT: Keepsake Books, 1991.

Cowley, Matthew. *Matthew Cowley Speaks: Discourses of Elder Matthew Cowley of the Quorum of the Twelve of the Church of Jesus Christ of Latter-day Saints.* Salt Lake City, UT: Deseret Book Company, 1954.

Dalrymple, G. Brent. *The Age of the Earth.* Stanford, CA: Stanford University Press, 1991.

Dellenbach, Robert K. "Hour of Conversion," *New Era*, June 2002.

DeMille, Cecil B. *BYU Speeches of the Year.* Provo, UT: Brigham Young University Press, May 1957.

Durham, G. Homer, ed. *The Gospel Kingdom: Selections from the Writings and Discourses of John Taylor, Third President of The Church of Jesus Christ of Latter-day Saints.* Salt Lake City, UT: Bookcraft, 1943.

—*Gospel Ideals: Selections from the Discourses of David O. McKay.* Salt Lake City, UT: Improvement Era, 1953.

Dibble, Philo. "Recollections of the Prophet Joseph Smith," *Juvenile Instructor,* June 1892.

Duffin, James G. "A Character Test," *Improvement Era,* February 1911.

Easton, M. G. *Illustrated Bible Dictionary.* Nashville: TN: Thomas Nelson, 1897.

"The Bondage of Sin," *Improvement Era,* February 1923.

Ehat, Andrew F. and Lyndon W. Cook. *The Words of Joseph Smith: The Contemporary Accounts of the Nauvoo Discourses of the Prophet Joseph.* Provo, UT: Religious Studies Center Brigham Young University, 1980.

Encarta World English Dictionary. New York, NY: St. Martins Press, 1999.

Eyring, Henry B. "Faith and the Oath and Covenant of the Priesthood," *Ensign*, May 2008.

Farley, S. Brent. "The Oath and Covenant of the Priesthood." *Sperry Symposium on the Doctrine and Covenants.* Salt Lake City: Desert Book, 1989.

First Presidency, "What is the Doctrine of the Priesthood?" Salt Lake City, UT: *Improvement Era,* February 1961.
Faust, James E. "A Royal Priesthood," *Ensign,* May 2006.
—*In the Strength of the Lord: The Life and Teachings of James E. Faust.* Salt Lake City, UT: Deseret Book, 1999.
—"He Healeth the Broken Heart," *Ensign* July 2005.
—"Our Search for Happiness, *Ensign,* Oct. 2000.
—"Standing in Holy Places," *Ensign,* May 2005.
—"The Devil's Throat," *Ensign,* May 2003.
—"The Gift of the Holy Ghost—A Sure Compass," *Ensign,* April 1996.
—"The Shield of Faith," *Ensign,* May 2000.
"Galaxy Map." Washington D.C.: The National Geographic Society, June 1983.
Galbraith, David B., D. Kelly Ogden, and Andrew C. Skinner. *Jerusalem—The Eternal City.* Salt Lake City, UT: Deseret Book, 1996.
Gardner, R. Quinn. "Becoming a Zion Society," *Ensign,* February 1979.
—"I Have a Question," *Ensign,* March 1978.
Gibbons, Ted L. *Be Not Afraid,* Springville, UT: Cedar Fort, Inc., 2009.
Goddard, Wallace H. "Blessed by Angels." *MeridianMagazine.com,* July 27, 2009.
—*Drawing Heaven into Your Marriage.* Fairfax, VA: Meridian Publishing, 2007.
Grant, Heber J. *Teachings of Presidents of the Church.* Salt Lake City, UT: The Church of Jesus Christ of Latter-day Saints, 2002.
Guralnik, David B., ed. *Webster's New World Dictionary, 2nd College Edition.* New York City, NY: The New World Publishing Company, 1970.
Hafen, Bruce C. *The Broken Heart: Applying the Atonement to Life's Experiences.* Salt Lake City, UT: Deseret Book, 1989.
Haight, David B. "The Sacrament and the Sacrifice," *Ensign,* November 1989.
Hamilton, Edith. *Spokesman for God.* New York, NY: Norton and Company, 1977.
Hinckley, Gordon B. "Blessed Are the Merciful," *Ensign,* May 1990.
—*Faith: The Essence of True Religion.* Salt Lake City, UT: Deseret Book, 1989.
—"Our Mission of Saving," *Ensign,* November 1991.
—"Priesthood: The Power of Godliness," *Improvement Era,* December 1970.
—*Stand a Little Taller.* Salt Lake City, UT: Eagle Gate, 2000.
—*Standing for Something.* New York, NY: Three Rivers Press, 2000.
—*Teachings of Gordon B. Hinckley.* Salt Lake City, UT: Deseret Book, 2002.
—"The Dawning of a Brighter Day," *Ensign,* May 2004.
—"The Stone Cut Out of the Mountain," *Ensign,* 2007.
—"Till We Meet Again," *Ensign,* November 2001.
—"We Thank Thee for This Sacred Structure," *Church News,* 8 November 1997.
— "Your Greatest Challenge, Mother," *Ensign,* November 2000.
Holland, Jeffrey R. "Broken Things to Mend," *Ensign,* May 2006.
—"However Long and Hard the Road," *Ensign,* September 2002.
—*On Earth As It Is in Heaven.* Salt Lake City, UT: Deseret Book, 1989.

Holzapfel, Richard Neitzel and Thomas A. Wayment, eds., *The Life and Teachings of Jesus Christ: From the Transfiguration through the Triumphant Entry.* Salt Lake City, UT: Deseret Book, 2006.

Horton, George A. "Abraham's Act of Faith Reflects 'a Soul Like Unto Our Savior,'" *LDS Church News,* April 2, 1994.

"'Hymn of the Pearl': an Ancient Counterpart To 'O My Father.'" *BYU Studies,* vol. 36, 1996–97.

Hymns of the Church of Jesus Christ of Latter-day Saints. Salt Lake City, UT: The Church of Jesus Christ of Latter-day Saints, 1985.

Jackson, Kent P. and Robert L. Millet. eds. *Studies in Scripture.* Salt Lake City, UT: Deseret Book 1989.

Jensen, Marlin K. "Living after the Manner of Happiness," *Ensign,* December 2002.

Jenson, Andrew, *Historical Record: A Monthly Periodical.* Salt Lake City, UT: Deseret News, 1886—1890.

Jessee, Dean. "Joseph Knight's Recollection of Early Mormon History." Provo, UT: *BYU Studies,* vol. 17, no. 1, 1976.

Johnson, Clark V. *Doctrines for Exaltation: The 1989 Sperry Symposium on the Doctrine and Covenants.* Salt Lake City, UT: Deseret Book, 1989.

Josephus. *Complete Works.* William Whiston, trans., Grand Rapids, MI: Kregal Publications, 1960.

Kimball, Spencer W. "A Gift of Gratitude," *Tambuli,* December 1977.

—"Becoming the Pure in Heart," *Ensign,* May 1978.

—*Faith Precedes the Miracle: Based on Discourses of Spencer W. Kimball.* Salt Lake City, UT: Deseret Book, 1972.

—"The Fruit of Our Welfare Services Labors," *Ensign,* November 1978.

—"The Role of Righteous Women," *Ensign,* November 1979.

—*The Teachings of Spencer W. Kimball.* Salt Lake City, UT: Bookcraft, 1982.

—"Welfare Services: The Gospel in Action," *Ensign,* November 1977.

—"Young Women Fireside 1981—In Love and Power and without Fear," *New Era,* July 1981.

Kirchhoff, Frederick. "Reconstruction of Self in Wordsworth's 'Ode on Intimations of Immortality from Recollections of Early Childhood.'" *Narcissism and the Text.* New York, NY: New York University Press, 1986.

Kirtland Council Minute Book, eds. Fred Collier and William S. Hartwell, Salt Lake City, UT: Collier's Publishing, 1996.

Largey, Dennis L. *Book of Mormon Reference Companion.* Salt Lake City, UT: Deseret Book, 2003.

Larsen, Dean L. "A Royal Generation," *Ensign,* May 1983.

Larson, Stan "The King Follett Discourse: a Newly Amalgamated Text." Provo, UT: *BYU Studies,* Vol. 18, 1977–1978.

Layton, Lynne and Schapiro, Barbara A. *Narcissism and the Text: Studies in Literature and the Psychology of Self.* New York, NY: New York University Press, 1986.

Lee, Harold B. *Decisions for Successful Living.* Salt Lake City, UT: Deseret Book, 1973.

—"Stand Ye in Holy Places," *Ensign,* July 1973.

—*The Teachings of Harold B. Lee.* Salt Lake City, UT: Deseret Book, 1974.

Lightner, Mary. Address to Brigham Young University. *BYU Archives and Manuscripts, Writings of Early Latter-day Saints,* 1905.

Ludlow, Daniel H. *A Companion to Your Study of the Book of Mormon.* Salt Lake City, UT: Deseret Book, 1976.

—*Encyclopedia of Mormonism.* New York City, NY: Macmillan Publishing, 1992.

Lund, Gerald N. *Jesus Christ, Key to the Plan of Salvation.* Salt Lake City, UT: Deseret Book, 1991.

—"Old Testament Types and Symbols," *A Witness of Jesus Christ: The 1989 Sperry Symposium on the Old Testament.* ed. Richard D. Draper, Salt Lake City, UT: Deseret Book, 1990.

Lundquist, John M. and Stephen D. Ricks, eds. *By Study and Also by Faith: Essays in Honor of Hugh W. Nibley on the Occasion of His Eightieth Birthday.* Provo, UT: Maxwell Institute, 1992.

Lundwall, N. B. *Temples of the Most High.* Salt Lake City, UT: Bookcraft, 1965.

"Map: Old Testament Stories: Part Two," *Deseret News.* Jan. 8, 1994.

Maxwell, Cory H., ed. *The Neal A. Maxwell Quote Book.* Salt Lake City, UT: Bookcraft, 1997.

Maxwell, Neal A. *A Wonderful Flood of Light.* Salt Lake City, UT: Deseret Book, 1991.

—*But for a Small Moment.* Salt Lake City, UT: Bookcraft, 1987.

—"Consecrate Thy Performance." *Ensign,* May 2002.

—*Disposition of a Disciple.* Salt Lake City, UT: Deseret Book, 1976.

—"Enduring Well," *Ensign,* April 1997.

—*Even As I Am.* Salt Lake City, UT: Deseret Book, 1991.

—*If Thou Endure It Well.* Salt Lake City, UT: Bookcraft, 2002.

—*Lord, Increase Our Faith.* Salt Lake City, UT: Bookcraft, 1994.

—*Men and Women of Christ.* Salt Lake City, UT: Deseret Book, 1991.

—*Notwithstanding My Weakness.* Salt Lake City, UT: Deseret Book, 1981.

—*One More Strain of Praise.* Salt Lake City, UT: Deseret Book, 2003.

—"Patience," *Ensign,* October 1980.

—*That Ye May Believe.* Salt Lake City, UT: Bookcraft, 1994.

—*The Promise of Discipleship.* Salt Lake City, UT: Deseret Book, 2001.

—"These Are Your Days," *New Era,* January 1985.

McConkie, Bruce R. *A New Witness for the Articles of Faith.* Salt Lake City, UT: Deseret Book, 1985.

—*Doctrinal New Testament Commentary.* Salt Lake City, UT: Deseret Book, 1972.

—*Doctrines of Salvation: Sermons and Writings of Joseph Fielding Smith,* Salt Lake City, UT: Bookcraft, 1954–1956.

—*Mormon Doctrine.* Salt Lake City, UT: Bookcraft: 1966.

—"Obedience, Consecration, and Sacrifice," *Ensign,* May 1975.

—"The Doctrine of the Priesthood," *Ensign,* May 1982.

—*The Mortal Messiah: From Bethlehem to Calvary.* Salt Lake City, UT: Deseret Book, 1981.

—"*The Probationary Test of Mortality.*" Address delivered at the University of Utah Institute, January 10, 1982.
—*The Promised Messiah: The First Coming of Christ.* Salt Lake City, UT: Deseret Book, 1981.
—"The Ten Blessings of the Priesthood," *Ensign,* November 1977.
McConkie, Joseph Fielding and Robert L. Millet. *Doctrinal Commentary on the Book of Mormon.* Salt Lake City, UT: Deseret Book, 1987–1993.
—*Joseph Smith: The Choice Seer.* Salt Lake City, UT: Bookcraft, 1996.
—*Revelations of the Restoration.* Salt Lake City, UT: Deseret Book, 2000.
McKay, David O. *Gospel Ideals: Selections from the Discourses of David O. McKay.* Salt Lake City, UT: Deseret Book, 1993.
----*Pathways to Happiness.* Salt Lake City, UT: Bookcraft, 1957.
McMullin, Keith B. "Come to Zion! Come to Zion!" Salt Lake City, UT: *Ensign,* November 2002.
Merriam Webster's New World Dictionary, Third Edition. New York, NY: Simon and Schuster, 1998
Middlemiss, Clare. *Man May Know for Himself: Teachings of President David O. McKay.* Salt Lake City, UT: Deseret Book, 1967.
Millet, Robert L. "Quest for the City of God: The Doctrine Of Zion In Modern Revelation," *1989 Sperry Symposium on the Doctrine and Covenants.* Salt Lake City, UT: Deseret Book, 1989.
—*The Capstone of Our Religion: Insights into the Doctrine and Covenants.* Salt Lake City, UT: Deseret Book, 1989.
—*The Life Beyond.* Salt Lake City, UT: Deseret Book, 1986.
—*The Power of the Word: Saving Doctrines from the Book of Mormon. Salt Lake City, UT: Deseret Book,* 2000.
Monson, Thomas S. "In Quest of the Abundant Life." *Ensign,* March 1988.
Nelson, Russell M. "Personal Priesthood Responsibility," *Ensign,* October 2005.
—*The Power within Us. Salt Lake City, UT: Deseret Book, 1989.*
Nelson, William O. "Enoch and His Message for Latter Days," *Deseret News,* Feb. 5, 1994.
Neuenschwander, Dennis. "Ordinances and Covenants," *Ensign,* August 2001.
Nibley, Hugh. *Abraham in Egypt.* Salt Lake City, UT and Provo, UT: Deseret Book and FARMS, 2000.
—*An Approach to the Book of Mormon.* Salt Lake City, UT: Deseret Book, 1988.
—*Approaching Zion.* Salt Lake City, UT: Deseret Book, 1989.
—"Educating the Saints—A Brigham Young Mosaic." Provo, UT: *BYU Studies,* Vol. 11, Autumn 1970.
—*Nibley on the Timely and the Timeless.* Provo, UT: Religious Studies Center, Brigham Young University, 2004.
—*Teachings of the Book of Mormon.* Provo, UT: Covenant Communications, 2004.
—*Temple and Cosmos: Beyond This Ignorant Present.* Salt Lake City, UT: Deseret Book, 1992.
Nibley, Preston. *Brigham Young: The Man and His Work,* 4th ed. Salt Lake City, UT: Deseret Book, 1960.

Nielsen, Donna B. *Beloved Bridegroom*. Salt Lake City, UT: Onyx Press, 1999.

Nyman, Monte S. and Charles D. Tate, Jr., eds. *Fourth Nephi through Moroni: From Zion to Destruction*. Salt Lake City, UT: Bookcraft, 1992.

—*The Capstone of Our Religion: Insights into the Doctrine and Covenants*. Salt Lake City, UT: Bookcraft, 1989.

Oaks, Dallin H. "Good, Better, Best," *Ensign*, November 2007.

—"He Heals the Heavy Laden," *Ensign*, November 2006

—"Preparation for the Second Coming," *Ensign*, November 2004.

—"Taking Upon Us the Name of Jesus Christ," *Ensign*, May 1985.

—"The Challenge to Become," *Ensign*, November 2000.

—"Timing," *Ensign*, October 2003.

Oaks, Robert C. "The Power of Patience," *Ensign*, November 2006.

Otten, L. G. and C. M. Caldwell. *Sacred Truths of the Doctrine and Covenants*. Salt Lake City, UT: Deseret Book, 1982–1983.

Pack, Frederick J. "Was the Earth Created in Six Days of Twenty-Four Hours Each?" *Improvement Era*, October 1930.

Packer, Boyd K. "Personal Revelation: The Gift, the Test, and the Promise," *Ensign*, November 1994.

—"Restoration," *First Worldwide Leadership Training Meeting*. Salt Lake City, UT: The Church of Jesus Christ of Latter-day Saints, January 2003.

—*That All May Be Edified*. Salt Lake City, UT: Bookcraft, 1982.

—"The Candle of the Lord," *Ensign*, January 1983.

—"The One Pure Defense (An Evening with President Boyd K. Packer)," Intellectual Reserve, 2004. Address to CES Religious Educators, 6 February 2004, Salt Lake Tabernacle.

Parry, Donald W., ed. *Temples of the Ancient World: Ritual and Symbolism*. Salt Lake City, UT and Provo, UT: Deseret and FARMS, 1994.

—*Understanding the Book of Revelation*. Salt Lake City, UT: Deseret Book, 1998.

Peterson, H. Burke. "Your Special Purpose," *New Era*, October 2001.

Pratt, Orson. *Times and Seasons*, vol. 6. no. 10, 1 June 1845.

Riddle, Chauncey C. "The New and Everlasting Covenant," 1989 *Sperry Symposium on the Doctrine and Covenants*. Salt Lake City: Desert Book, 1989.

Roberts, B.H. *Comprehensive History of the Church of Jesus Christ of Latter-day Saints*. Salt Lake City, UT: Church of Jesus Christ of Latter-day Saints, 1930.

—*Seventy's Course of Theology*. Salt Lake City, UT: Deseret Book, 1931.

Romney, Marion G. "Church Welfare Services' Basic Principles," *Ensign*, May 1976.

—"Church Welfare—Temporal Service in a Spiritual Setting," *Ensign*, May 1980

—"Priesthood," *Ensign*, May 1982.

—"'In Mine Own Way,'" *Ensign*, November 1976.

—"The Celestial Nature of Self-reliance," *Ensign*, November 1982.

—"The Oath and Covenant Which Belongeth to the Priesthood," *Ensign*, November 1980.

—"The Purpose of Church Welfare Services," *Ensign*, May 1977.

—"The Royal Law of Love," *Ensign*, May 1978.
—"Unity," *Ensign*, May 1983.
—"Welfare Services: The Savior's Program," *Ensign*, October 1980.
Salt Lake School of the Prophets Minutes. Salt Lake City, UT: The Church of Jesus Christ of Latter-day Saints, 1899.
"Sermon Given to Different People," *LDS Church News*, Feb. 18, 1995.
Skidmore, Rex A. "What Part Should a Teenager Play in a Family?" *Improvement Era*, 1952.
Skinner, Andrew C. *Temple Worship: 20 Truths That Will Bless Your Life*. Salt Lake City, UT: Deseret Book, 2008.
—*The Old Testament and the Latter-Day Saints*. Salt Lake City, UT: Deseret Book, 2005.
Smith, Hyrum M. and Janne M. Sjodahl. *Doctrine and Covenants Commentary*. Salt Lake City, UT: Deseret Book, 1960.
Smith, Joseph. *Evening and Morning Star*, July, 1833.
—*History of The Church of Jesus Christ of Latter-day Saints*. Salt Lake City, UT: Deseret Book, 1980.
—*Lectures on Faith*. Salt Lake City, UT: Deseret Book, 1993.
Smith, Joseph F. *Gospel Doctrine: Selections from the Sermons and Writings of Joseph F. Smith*. Deseret News Press, 1919.
—*Teachings of Presidents of the Church*. Salt Lake City, UT: The Church of Jesus Christ of Latter-day Saints, 1998.
Smith, Joseph Fielding. *Church History and Modern Revelation*. Salt Lake City, UT: The Church of Jesus Christ of Latter-day Saints, 1946.
—"Our responsibility as Priesthood Holders," *Ensign*, June 1971.
—*Teachings of the Prophet Joseph Smith*. Salt Lake City, UT: Deseret Book, 1938.
—"The Duties of the Priesthood in Temple Work," *The Utah Genealogical and Historical Magazine*, vol. 30, no. 1, January 1939.
—*The Restoration of All Things*. Salt Lake City, UT: Deseret News Press, 1945.
Snow, Lorenzo. *The Teachings of Lorenzo Snow*, Salt Lake City, UT: Bookcraft, 1984.
Sorensen, A. D. "No Respector of Persons: Equality in the Kingdom," ed. Mary E. Stoval, *.As Women of Faith: Talks Selected from the BYU Women's Conferences*. Salt Lake City, UT: Deseret Book, 1989, 55.
Stevenson, Edward. "Life and History of Elder Edward Stevenson." Provo, UT: Special Collections, Harold B. Lee Library, Brigham Young University, n.d.
Stuy, Brian H., comp., *Collected Discourses*. Burbank, CA: B.H.S. Publishing, 1988.
Summerhays, James T. "The Stripling Elect." *MeridianMagazine.com*, February 20, 2009.
Talmage, James E. *Articles of Faith*. Salt Lake City, UT: Deseret Book, 1984.
—*Jesus the Christ*. Salt Lake City: Deseret News Press, 1915.
—"The Eternity of Sex," *Young Woman's Journal*, October 1914.
—*The House of the Lord*. Salt Lake City, UT: Bookcraft, 1962.
Tanakh: A New Translation of the Holy Scriptures According to the Traditional Hebrew Text. Philadelphia, PA: Jewish Publication Society of America, November 1985.
Tanner, N. Eldon. "Constancy Amid Change," Ensign, November 1979.

Tanner, Susan W. "All Things Shall Work Together for Your Good," *Ensign*, May 2004.
—"My Soul Delighteth in the Things of the Lord," *Ensign*, 2008.
Taylor, John. *Teachings of the Latter-day Prophets*. Salt Lake City, UT: Bookcraft, 1998.
Times and Seasons, vol. 6. no. 10, 1 June 1845.
Thomas, M. Catherine. "Alma the Younger, Part 1," Provo, UT: Neal A. Maxwell Institute for Religious Scholarship, 1996.
—"Alma the Younger, Part 2," Provo, UT: Neal A. Maxwell Institute for Religious Scholarship, 1996.
—"Benjamin and the Mysteries of God," *King Benjamin's Speech*. Provo, UT: Foundation for Ancient Research and Mormon Studies, 1998.
Turner, Rodney. *Woman and the Priesthood*. Salt Lake City, UT: Deseret Book, 1972.
Tvedtnes, John A. *The Church of the Old Testament*. Salt Lake City, UT: Deseret Book, 1967.
—"They Have Their Reward," *MeridianMagazine.com*, February 21, 2007.
Van Orden, Bruce A. and Brent L. Top. *Doctrines of the Book of Mormon: The 1991 Sperry Symposium*, Provo, UT: Maxwell Institute, 1993.
Watt, George D., ed. *Journal of Discourses*. Liverpool, England: F.D. Richards, et al., 1854–1886.
Whitney, Newell K. in *Messenger and Advocate*, 3 September 1837.
Whitney, Orson F. *Gospel Themes*. Salt Lake City, UT: n.p., 1914.
—*Life of Heber C. Kimball*. Salt Lake City, UT: Bookcraft, 1975.
—*Saturday Night Thoughts*. Salt Lake City, UT: Deseret News, 1927.
Wickman, Lance B. "Today," *Ensign*, May 2008.
Widtsoe, John A. *An Understandable Religion*. Salt Lake City, UT: The Church of Jesus Christ of Latter-day Saints, 1944.
—*Priesthood and Church Government*. Salt Lake City, UT: Deseret Book, 1939.
—*Utah Genealogical and Historical Magazine*. Salt Lake City, UT: October 1934.
Williams, Clyde J. *The Teachings of Lorenzo Snow, Fifth President of the Church of Jesus Christ of Latter-day Saints*. Salt Lake City, UT: Bookcraft, 1984.
Wilson, Marvin. *Our Father Abraham*, Grand Rapids, MI: Eerdmans Publishing Co., 1989.
Winder, Barbara W. "Finding Joy in Life," *Ensign*, November 1987.
Wirthlin, Joseph B. "The Great Commandment," *Ensign*, November 2007.
—"The Law of the Fast," *Ensign*, May 2001.
Woodruff, Wilford. *The Discourses of Wilford Woodruff*. Salt Lake City, UT: Bookcraft, 1946.
Yarn, David H. *The Gospel: God, Man, and Truth*. Salt Lake City, UT: Deseret Book, 1965.
Yorgason, Blaine M. *I Need Thee Every Hour*. Salt Lake City, UT: Deseret Book, 2003.
—*Spiritual Progression in the Last Days*. Salt Lake City, UT: Deseret Book, 1994.
Young, Brigham in *Deseret News*, 10 October 1866.
—*Discourses of Brigham Young*. Salt Lake City, UT: Deseret Book, 1926.
—*Journal History*. 28 September 1846.
—*Millennial Star, Vol. 16*. Salt Lake City, UT: The Church of Jesus Christ of Latter-day Saints, 1840–1970.

Index and Concordance

This is a master index of the book series. The page number is specific to the book in which it is located. For example: 101:3 means page 101 in book 3. Marker "P" refers to Portrait of a Zion Person.

Aaronic Priesthood. *See* **Oath and Covenant of the Priesthood;** *See* **Patriarchal Order of the Priesthood;** *See* **Priesthood**
    40:2, 41:2, 12:3, 22:3, 23:3, 36:3, 39:3, 42:3, 59:3, 60:3, 76:3, 92:3, 93:3, 103:3, 104:3, 202:3, 204:3, 50:4, 131:5

abundance
    5:6, 8:6, 10:6, 13:6, 17:6, 18:6, 31:6, 41:6, 44:6, 46:6, 52:6, 70:6, 82:6, 87:6, 96:6, 101:6, 103:6, 106:6, 107:6, 110:6, 111:6, 112:6, 114:6, 115:6

Adam
    empowered to become a savior to his family
        11:1

adultery. *See also* **immoral**
    Babylon distinguished by
        50:2

adversary. *See also* **devil;** *See also* **hell;** *See also* **Lucifer;** *See also* **Satan**
    attacks Saints more viciously than others
        44:1

adversity. *See also* **opposition;** *See also* **trial(s)**
    33:2, 51:2, 54:2, 56:2, 58:2, 61:2, 34:3, 66:3, 117:3, 132:3, 186:3, 178:4, 10:5, 27:5, 30:5, 76:5, 50:6, 101:6

affluence. *See also* **mammon;** *See also* **riches;** *See also* **wealth**
    85:1, 139:4, 103:5, 64:6, 71:6

agency
    a discussion of
        62–68:4

Amulek
    52:1, 80:1, 51:2, 52:2, 55:3, 42:4, 59:4, 133:4, 180:4, 36:5, 71:5, 56:6, 104:6

angels
    involved in crucible experiences
        26:5

anger. *See also* **contention**
    19:1, 57:1, 64:1, 75:1, 86:1, 87:1, 93:1, 96:1, 97:1, 98:1, 55:2, 23:3, 152:3, 169:3, 176:3, 5:4, 29:4, 34:4, 101:4, 111:4, 116:4, 121:4, 136:4, 165:4, 179:4, 180:4, 4:5, 15:5, 22:5, 41:5, 46:5, 79:5, 104:5, 107:5, 124:5, 17:6, 28:6, 34:6, 39:6, 60:6, 94:6, 116:6

anti-Christ
    17:P, 21:1, 49:1, 50:1, 51:1, 61:1, 79:1, 84:1, 85:1, 101:1, 54:2, 67:3, 87:4, 127:4, 175:4, 176:4, 33:5, 48:5, 7:6, 47:6, 88:6

apostasy
    27:1, 33:1, 34:1, 60:1, 68:1, 84:4, 108:5

apostle
    59:1, 17:2

Index & Concordance

Atonement
> 6:P, 14:P, 15:P, 24:P, 42:P, 11:1, 12:1, 22:1, 23:1, 42:1, 45:1, 47:1, 66:1, 70:1, 1:2, 3:2, 6:2, 7:2, 9:2, 10:2, 16:2, 17:2, 18:2, 19:2, 20:2, 23:2, 24:2, 25:2, 26:2, 27:2, 28:2, 29:2, 30:2, 31:2, 32:2, 34:2, 35:2, 36:2, 37:2, 38:2, 39:2, 45:2, 55:2, 57:2, 66:2, 67:2, 72:2, 93:2, 98:2, 1:3, 10:3, 17:3, 20:3, 21:3, 35:3, 63:3, 70:3, 73:3, 76:3, 158:3, 180:3, 196:3, 211:3, 214:3, 1:4, 16:4, 18:4, 19:4, 20:4, 31:4, 41:4, 42:4, 56:4, 57:4, 59:4, 64:4, 99:4, 122:4, 162:4, 185:4, 1:5, 4:5, 29:5, 64:5, 84:5, 87:5, 91:5, 106:5, 107:5, 111:5, 113:5, 117:5, 129:5, 133:5, 137:5, 15:6, 42:6, 67:6, 75:6

Babel
> a counterfeit gate of God
>> 54:1
>
> Nimrod established kingdom in
>> 53:1

Babylon. *See also* **world**
> a discussion of
>> 49–105:1
>
> state of mind defined by excess, self-indulgence
>> 54:1

baptism
> 2:P, 18:P, 21:P, 25:P, 11:1, 19:1, 23:1, 9:2, 18:2, 19:2, 21:2, 28:2, 31:2, 33:2, 34:2, 35:2, 36:2, 37:2, 38:2, 40:2, 41:2, 44:2, 45:2, 49:2, 53:2, 60:2, 63:2, 64:2, 67:2, 68:2, 70:2, 73:2, 75:2, 81:2, 82:2, 91:2, 93:2, 98:2, 1:3, 2:3, 4:3, 5:3, 9:3, 10:3, 11:3, 17:3, 21:3, 23:3, 27:3, 39:3, 42:3, 66:3, 70:3, 71:3, 76:3, 80:3, 93:3, 99:3, 117:3, 143:3, 144:3, 153:3, 179:3, 187:3, 193:3, 200:3, 210:3, 214:3, 1:4, 14:4, 26:4, 39:4, 51:4, 52:4, 88:4, 142:4, 144:4, 145:4, 1:5, 17:5, 18:5, 60:5, 61:5, 62:5, 63:5, 82:5, 83:5, 106:5, 117:5, 133:5, 134:5, 135:5, 68:6, 75:6, 76:6, 106:6

Beatitudes. *See also* **Sermon on the Mount**
> 16:P, 18:P, 28:P, 28:1, 49:3, 41:5, 82:5

believe. *See* **faith**
> in order to see
>> 68:5

Beloved Son. *See also* **Christ**; *See also* **Exemplar**; *See also* **Jehovah**; *See also* **Lamb**; *See also* **Savior**
> 47:1, 65:3, 111:3, 55:5, 56:5, 110:5, 115:5

Bible
> 39:1, 63:1, 83:1, 54:2, 7:3, 138:3, 153:3, 203:3, 8:5

blasphemy
> 59:1, 82:3

bloodline
> men ordained to priesthood regardless of
>> 17:1

Book of Mormon
> 12:P, 19:P, 21:P, 30:P, 39:P, 42:P, 1:1, 2:1, 5:1, 12:1, 17:1, 31:1, 34:1, 37:1, 61:1, 64:1, 67:1, 70:1, 78:1, 103:1, 18:2, 51:2, 7:3, 17:3, 19:3, 45:3, 46:3, 69:3, 70:3, 92:3, 120:3, 123:3, 132:3, 141:3, 146:3, 153:3, 163:3, 171:3, 180:3, 5:4, 26:4, 40:4, 69:4, 85:4, 97:4, 99:4, 104:4, 108:4, 124:4, 135:4, 138:4, 139:4, 157:4, 161:4, 4:5, 8:5, 11:5, 23:5, 34:5, 59:5, 78:5, 96:5, 103:5, 109:5, 118:5, 127:5, 129:5, 11:6, 15:6, 20:6, 25:6, 44:6, 59:6, 61:6, 63:6, 113:6

Bridegroom. *See also* **Christ, Jesus**
> 75:1, 85:1, 58:2, 71:2, 72:2, 73:2, 74:2, 75:2, 76:2, 77:2, 78:2, 79:2, 80:2, 81:2, 82:2, 83:2, 84:2, 85:2, 86:2, 87:2, 88:2, 89:2, 90:2, 91:2, 92:2, 93:2, 94:2, 95:2, 96:2, 97:2, 98:2, 111:3, 161:3, 173:3, 183:3, 98:4, 11:6

Brigham Young
> 14:P, 26:P, 39:P, 41:P, 3:1, 5:1, 6:1, 12:1, 39:1, 40:1, 44:1, 46:1, 90:1, 103:1, 1:2, 61:2, 1:3, 3:3, 19:3, 56:3, 96:3, 101:3, 102:3, 127:3, 128:3, 142:3, 164:3, 192:3, 193:3, 201:3, 214:3, 1:4, 10:4, 30:4, 47:4, 62:4, 75:4, 85:4, 87:4, 89:4, 97:4, 105:4, 106:4, 109:4, 113:4, 125:4, 131:4, 132:4, 133:4, 135:4, 137:4, 140:4, 141:4, 149:4, 150:4, 152:4, 1:5, 4:5, 11:5, 28:5, 41:5, 56:5, 73:5, 81:5, 84:5, 90:5, 91:5, 96:5, 97:5, 99:5, 101:5, 109:5, 127:5, 134:5, 136:5, 137:5, 11:6, 20:6, 21:6, 27:6, 30:6, 31:6, 45:6, 55:6, 56:6, 57:6, 58:6, 59:6, 61:6, 64:6, 65:6, 71:6, 105:6

brother of Jared
> 13:1, 74:1, 58:2, 184:3, 196:3, 209:3, 210:3, 8:5, 21:5, 29:5, 32:5, 34:5, 41:5, 43:5, 53:5, 58:5, 66:5, 68:5, 69:5, 70:5, 73:5, 86:5, 112:5, 119:5

Bruce R. McConkie
> 34:P, 36:P, 37:P, 11:1, 45:1, 85:2, 93:2, 2:3, 9:3, 11:3, 14:3, 21:3, 25:3, 33:3, 79:3, 214:3, 2:4, 8:4, 62:4, 68:4, 82:4, 135:4, 2:5, 7:5, 60:5, 64:5, 129:5, 58:6

business. *See* **mammon**

Cain
> 13:1, 51:1, 52:1, 53:1, 54:1, 61:1, 69:1, 72:1, 74:1, 77:1, 79:1, 90:1, 101:1, 109:3, 82:4, 127:4, 150:4, 175:4, 176:4, 47:6, 88:6

calling and election made sure
> chronology of
>> 83:3

carnal
> 20:P, 25:P, 41:P, 19:1, 23:1, 59:1, 62:1, 70:1, 89:1, 94:1, 101:1, 102:1, 8:2, 23:2, 25:2, 29:2, 33:2, 62:2, 23:3, 109:3, 172:3, 178:3, 64:4, 65:4, 100:4, 109:4, 149:4, 14:5, 44:5, 67:5, 93:5, 16:6, 26:6, 76:6

celestial kingdom
> 14:P, 16:P, 18:P, 22:P, 28:P, 34:P, 48:1, 14:2, 15:2, 16:2, 18:2, 21:2, 27:2, 37:2, 74:2, 2:3, 22:3, 23:3, 28:3, 34:3, 69:3, 71:3, 79:3, 103:3, 115:3, 121:3, 124:3, 125:3, 153:3, 168:3, 182:3, 186:3, 199:3, 2:4, 3:4, 4:4, 6:4, 8:4, 10:4, 15:4, 26:4, 29:4, 30:4, 38:4, 51:4, 52:4, 54:4, 63:4, 68:4, 73:4, 77:4, 79:4, 89:4, 90:4, 91:4, 95:4, 126:4, 132:4, 141:4, 144:4, 148:4, 150:4, 152:4, 185:4, 2:5, 11:5, 31:5, 50:5, 78:5, 120:5, 132:5, 134:5, 135:5, 3:6, 6:6, 9:6, 13:6, 31:6, 46:6, 56:6, 66:6, 68:6, 72:6, 94:6, 105:6, 110:6

charity
    a discussion of
        165–184:4
    characteristics of
        147–173:3

chaste
    5:2, 22:2, 66:2, 24:5, 57:5

Christ, Jesus. *See also* **Beloved Son**; *See also* **Exemplar**; *See also* **Jehovah**; *See also* **Lamb**; *See also* **Savior**
    a discussion of
        as Bridegroom
            72–98:2
        coming into his presence
            77:2
        taking name of, upon us
            59:2
    frees us from the powers of Babylon
        26:1

city of Enoch
    14:1, 16:1, 36:1, 5:3, 19:3, 23:5, 34:5, 72:5, 2:6

comforter. *See also* **Holy Ghost**
    37:2, 86:2, 71:3

commerce. *See also* **mammon**
    76:1, 79:1

compete, competition
    79:1, 88:1, 119:3, 132:3

consecrate, consecration
    a discussion of
        blessings of living
            33–50:4
        characteristics of the law of
            3–31:4
        guiding principles of
            62–91:4
    living law of, brings blessings of abundance
        18:1
    to set apart
        160:4

contention. *See also* **anger**
    6:P, 12:P, 43:P, 19:1, 21:1, 24:1, 29:1, 64:1, 67:1, 79:1, 85:1, 88:1, 102:1, 8:3, 119:3, 128:3, 42:4, 48:4, 179:4, 180:4, 4:5, 43:5, 102:5, 103:5, 104:5, 107:5, 108:5, 2:6, 117:6

cooperate
>25:P, 6:2, 9:2, 100:5

corn
>kernel of, represents potential of grace freely given
>>55:3

coronation
>1:2, 9:2, 98:2, 29:3, 30:3, 36:3, 184:3, 194:3, 195:3, 65:5, 73:5, 135:5

counterfeit
>Satan always has, to God's works
>>61:1

covet
>36:P, 24:1, 70:1, 69:4, 86:4, 100:4, 102:4, 148:4, 16:6, 17:6, 18:6, 115:6

Creator. *See* **Christ, Jesus**

crown. *See* **coronation**

crucibles
>angels involved in
>>26:5
>
>many, last fourteen years
>>25:5

deceive. *See* **deception**

deception
>victims of, will not be condemned
>>22:1

Deity. *See* **God**

deliverance
>20:P, 18:1, 25:1, 72:1, 8:2, 22:2, 35:2, 51:2, 52:2, 26:3, 121:3, 128:3, 140:3, 148:3, 44:4, 84:4, 125:4, 131:4, 161:4, 162:4, 163:4, 174:4, 178:4, 180:4, 185:4, 3:5, 16:5, 17:5, 19:5, 23:5, 26:5, 27:5, 29:5, 36:5, 38:5, 39:5, 40:5, 45:5, 48:5, 49:5, 50:5, 51:5, 52:5, 55:5, 57:5, 68:5, 69:5, 70:5, 71:5, 72:5, 73:5, 75:5, 76:5, 78:5, 45:6, 52:6, 101:6

descend
>we must, below all things to ascend above all
>>39:1

devil. *See also* **adversary;** *See also* **hell;** *See also* **Lucifer;** *See also* **Satan**
>6:P, 35:P, 41:P, 21:1, 24:1, 44:1, 51:1, 52:1, 60:1, 61:1, 62:1, 63:1, 64:1, 68:1, 70:1, 72:1, 73:1, 84:1, 86:1, 90:1, 92:1, 100:1, 101:1, 102:1, 28:2, 32:2, 49:2, 89:2, 98:2, 97:3, 109:3, 131:3, 160:3, 163:3, 172:3, 188:3, 189:3, 19:4, 45:4, 63:4, 64:4, 65:4, 67:4, 70:4, 109:4, 113:4, 120:4, 138:4, 141:4, 149:4, 151:4, 152:4, 14:5, 18:5, 47:5, 55:5, 101:5, 104:5, 107:5, 120:5, 26:6, 27:6, 30:6, 38:6, 63:6, 65:6, 71:6, 117:6

disputations
>6:P, 17:P, 26:P, 30:1, 49:1, 57:1, 19:3, 42:4, 119:4, 107:5, 108:5, 109:5, 122:5, 2:6, 37:6, 117:6

Index & Concordance

elect
>57:1, 63:1, 85:1, 101:1, 103:1, 43:2, 48:2, 92:2, 40:3, 63:3, 79:3, 80:3, 81:3, 82:3, 84:3, 85:3, 87:3, 105:3, 114:3, 140:3, 154:3, 203:3, 73:5, 74:5, 90:5, 96:5, 7:6

Elijah
>23:P, 35:P, 31:1, 81:2, 12:3, 13:3, 14:3, 15:3, 16:3, 17:3, 65:3, 116:3, 121:3, 66:4, 130:4, 8:5, 51:5, 70:5, 92:5, 52:6

Eliza R. Snow
>34:1

endow, endowment
>>Abraham administered, regardless of bloodline
>>>17:1

Enoch
>3:P, 12:P, 15:P, 33:P, 37:P, 39:P, 3:1, 4:1, 6:1, 7:1, 13:1, 14:1, 15:1, 16:1, 18:1, 32:1, 33:1, 36:1, 37:1, 55:1, 58:1, 74:1, 87:1, 88:1, 103:1, 11:2, 12:2, 5:3, 7:3, 9:3, 18:3, 19:3, 20:3, 24:3, 25:3, 27:3, 30:3, 46:3, 57:3, 72:3, 73:3, 89:3, 93:3, 116:3, 184:3, 198:3, 204:3, 207:3, 208:3, 209:3, 10:4, 11:4, 82:4, 86:4, 157:4, 23:5, 34:5, 37:5, 69:5, 72:5, 86:5, 89:5, 90:5, 94:5, 96:5, 100:5, 101:5, 112:5, 124:5, 125:5, 127:5, 132:5, 1:6, 2:6

equal
>6:P, 7:P, 12:P, 33:P, 27:1, 41:1, 57:1, 65:1, 87:1, 13:2, 64:2, 4:3, 18:3, 40:3, 41:3, 50:3, 60:3, 90:3, 105:3, 106:3, 119:3, 132:3, 200:3, 9:4, 24:4, 26:4, 27:4, 30:4, 36:4, 37:4, 38:4, 39:4, 49:4, 58:4, 59:4, 61:4, 73:4, 74:4, 77:4, 90:4, 96:4, 125:4, 156:4, 183:4, 185:4, 4:5, 122:5, 123:5, 3:6, 10:6, 45:6, 53:6, 77:6, 107:6, 116:6

exalt
>25:P, 1:2, 9:2, 32:2, 33:2, 45:2, 54:2, 57:2, 61:2, 28:3, 59:3, 132:3, 134:3, 142:3, 146:3, 4:4, 37:4, 52:4, 56:4, 109:4, 184:4, 93:5, 26:6, 76:6, 78:6, 108:6, 116:6

Exemplar. *See also* **Christ, Jesus;** *See also* **Jehovah;** *See also* **Lamb;** *See also* **Savior**
>39:1, 65:3

Ezra Taft Benson
>34:P, 8:1, 24:1, 41:1, 61:1, 67:1, 26:3, 109:3, 116:3, 205:3, 6:4, 15:4, 25:4, 26:4, 27:4, 28:4, 48:4, 59:4, 1:6, 80:6, 105:6

face-to-face
>>coming, with God is ultimate blessing and right of Zion people
>>>97:3

family, families
>3:P, 4:P, 23:P, 27:P, 29:P, 31:P, 32:P, 33:P, 34:P, 36:P, 37:P, 38:P, 42:P, 43:P, 6:1, 11:1, 12:1, 13:1, 14:1, 17:1, 18:1, 24:1, 26:1, 40:1, 42:1, 43:1, 45:1, 47:1, 54:1, 89:1, 93:1, 5:2, 23:2, 29:2, 32:2, 36:2, 37:2, 41:2, 50:2, 51:2, 52:2, 53:2, 62:2, 64:2, 68:2, 80:2, 83:2, 92:2, 5:3, 8:3, 12:3, 13:3, 14:3, 15:3, 16:3, 17:3, 20:3, 25:3, 26:3, 27:3, 28:3, 31:3, 32:3, 34:3, 65:3, 69:3, 70:3, 76:3, 78:3, 92:3, 100:3, 111:3, 113:3, 120:3, 136:3, 139:3, 146:3, 170:3, 178:3, 185:3, 186:3, 199:3, 200:3, 201:3, 204:3, 206:3, 207:3, 212:3, 4:4, 6:4, 8:4, 9:4, 23:4, 26:4, 27:4, 29:4, 30:4, 39:4, 41:4, 69:4, 72:4, 73:4,

74:4, 79:4, 82:4, 84:4, 86:4, 87:4, 133:4, 134:4, 141:4, 151:4, 157:4, 170:4, 171:4, 179:4, 180:4, 4:5, 21:5, 24:5, 42:5, 50:5, 51:5, 52:5, 62:5, 66:5, 71:5, 94:5, 95:5, 104:5, 107:5, 127:5, 133:5, 134:5, 5:6, 57:6, 65:6, 78:6, 87:6, 98:6, 102:6, 103:6, 104:6, 111:6, 112:6, 113:6, 114:6, 115:6

fathers
    6:P, 18:1, 28:1, 35:1, 45:1, 63:1, 81:1, 91:1, 98:1, 32:2, 75:2, 13:3, 15:3, 17:3, 23:3, 27:3, 65:3, 77:3, 91:3, 104:3, 160:3, 161:3, 207:3, 118:4, 124:4, 128:4, 137:4, 141:4, 152:4, 67:5, 109:5, 124:5, 128:5, 136:5, 4:6, 37:6, 43:6, 48:6, 60:6, 66:6

fear
    11:P, 26:P, 29:P, 42:P, 43:P, 23:1, 35:1, 37:1, 40:1, 53:1, 56:1, 64:1, 84:1, 85:1, 93:1, 94:1, 97:1, 59:2, 86:2, 39:3, 128:3, 130:3, 142:3, 149:3, 158:3, 169:3, 186:3, 196:3, 4:4, 22:4, 116:4, 141:4, 171:4, 172:4, 177:4, 27:5, 37:5, 57:5, 101:5, 133:5, 1:6, 35:6, 66:6, 90:6, 97:6, 98:6, 112:6

flatter
    73:1, 96:1

forgive
    10:P, 39:2, 40:2, 116:4, 178:4, 183:4, 35:6, 101:6

fornication
    56:1, 57:1, 58:1, 59:1, 76:1, 80:1, 93:1, 50:2, 22:5

fourteen years
    many crucibles last
        25:5

fruit
    ripe, falls from tree of life to rot on ground
        96:1

fundamentalism
    definition of
        83:1

Gadianton robbers. *See also* **secret combinations**
    97:1

Garden of Eden
    13:1, 77:1, 108:4, 8:5, 28:5, 36:5, 72:5, 25:6

gathering
    always associated with Zion
        20:1

generosity. *See* **selflessness**

give yourself rich. *See* **abundance**
    8:P, 176:4, 89:6

God-like, godliness
    become, by learning how to lift others
        5:1

Index & Concordance

gold
> 28:P, 38:P, 42:P, 27:1, 50:1, 52:1, 58:1, 59:1, 62:1, 76:1, 96:1, 22:2, 80:2, 94:2, 129:3, 151:3, 9:4, 40:4, 44:4, 82:4, 101:4, 103:4, 106:4, 109:4, 116:4, 118:4, 124:4, 132:4, 139:4, 140:4, 145:4, 146:4, 3:5, 21:5, 23:5, 24:5, 25:5, 26:5, 17:6, 19:6, 22:6, 27:6, 35:6, 36:6, 44:6, 55:6, 64:6, 65:6, 68:6, 69:6, 70:6

good
> definition of
>> 9:1

goods. *See* **mammon**

Gordon B. Hinckley
> 6:P, 7:1, 28:2, 55:3, 172:3, 211:3, 37:4, 40:4, 41:4, 56:4, 59:4, 60:4, 164:4, 170:4, 87:5, 78:6, 83:6, 93:6

grace. *See also* **mercy**
> 15:P, 19:P, 22:P, 4:1, 6:1, 10:1, 11:1, 28:1, 42:1, 4:2, 17:2, 18:2, 19:2, 20:2, 22:2, 23:2, 26:2, 29:2, 36:2, 38:2, 43:2, 45:2, 78:2, 16:3, 21:3, 24:3, 52:3, 53:3, 54:3, 55:3, 60:3, 64:3, 86:3, 104:3, 153:3, 198:3, 200:3, 57:4, 66:4, 79:4, 89:4, 92:4, 139:4, 146:4, 174:4, 175:4, 177:4, 181:4, 184:4, 7:5, 20:5, 31:5, 32:5, 45:5, 90:5, 124:5, 64:6, 70:6, 75:6, 80:6, 81:6, 82:6, 83:6, 89:6, 90:6, 100:6, 101:6

Harold B. Lee
> 16:P, 28:P, 28:1, 82:1, 49:3, 130:3, 131:3, 204:3, 82:5, 147:5

heal
> 21:P, 1:1, 2:1, 46:1, 135:3, 142:3, 152:3, 165:3, 171:3, 73:4, 77:4, 142:4, 144:4, 159:4, 160:4, 161:4, 184:4, 15:5, 113:5, 68:6, 86:6

healing
> we prepare for Zion by experiencing
>> 160:4

health
> 23:P, 9:1, 76:1, 90:1, 100:1, 24:2, 29:2, 123:3, 18:4, 161:4, 180:4, 185:4, 15:5, 24:5, 25:5, 37:5, 57:5, 71:5, 72:5, 1:6, 86:6, 103:6, 109:6

heart
> a discussion of
>> pure in
>>> 77–108:5
> is altar of soul
>> 49:5
> must be changed to attain Zion
>> 12:1

Heber C. Kimball
> 114:1, 83:3, 100:3, 101:3, 148:5

heir
> 11:1, 53:1, 101:1, 29:3, 76:3, 195:3, 45:5

hell. *See also* **adversary;** *See also* **devil;** *See also* **Lucifer;** *See also* **Satan**
18:P, 41:P, 47:1, 63:1, 68:1, 70:1, 72:1, 73:1, 74:1, 101:1, 102:1, 26:2, 97:3, 109:3, 128:3, 131:3, 154:3, 160:3, 163:3, 188:3, 75:4, 109:4, 112:4, 113:4, 120:4, 126:4, 141:4, 149:4, 13:5, 14:5, 47:5, 56:5, 97:5, 5:6, 26:6, 29:6, 30:6, 39:6, 46:6, 65:6

Holy Ghost. *See also* **comforter**
presence of, signifies we are retaining remission of sins
38:2

homosexuality
56:1

Hugh Nibley
5:P, 26:P, 33:P, 5:1, 7:1, 8:1, 33:1, 34:1, 50:1, 51:1, 56:1, 57:1, 70:1, 71:1, 75:1, 77:1, 79:1, 80:1, 89:1, 92:1, 93:1, 47:3, 109:3, 110:3, 137:3, 6:4, 7:4, 16:4, 28:4, 50:4, 56:4, 85:4, 87:4, 93:4, 94:4, 98:4, 99:4, 105:4, 108:4, 110:4, 113:4, 127:4, 132:4, 136:4, 138:4, 150:4, 21:5, 22:5, 96:5, 7:6, 8:6, 12:6, 15:6, 21:6, 25:6, 27:6, 30:6, 47:6, 56:6, 59:6, 61:6, 105:6, 116:6

hundredfold
8:P, 25:2, 27:2, 29:2, 123:3, 126:3, 127:3, 141:3, 151:3, 36:4, 58:4, 67:4, 92:4, 145:4, 153:4, 170:4, 177:4, 184:4, 70:5, 118:5, 3:6, 6:6, 69:6, 70:6, 72:6, 87:6, 89:6, 106:6, 107:6, 108:6, 109:6, 110:6

husband. *See also* **marriage**
24:2, 66:2, 75:2, 76:2, 77:2, 78:2, 79:2, 80:2, 81:2, 83:2, 84:2, 85:2, 89:2, 90:2, 94:2, 97:2, 13:3, 15:3, 17:3, 23:3, 59:3, 64:3, 85:3, 110:3, 136:3, 179:3, 183:3, 198:3, 211:3, 41:4, 43:4, 98:4, 155:4, 156:4, 157:4, 42:5, 117:5, 11:6

hypocrisy
80:1, 41:2, 44:3, 47:3, 108:3, 110:3, 119:3, 159:3, 160:3, 165:3, 167:3, 140:4, 64:6

idleness
38:P, 27:1, 56:1, 119:3, 129:3, 20:4, 39:4, 83:4, 84:4, 85:4, 86:4, 101:4, 121:4, 157:4, 18:6, 41:6, 50:6

idolatrous
54:1, 88:1, 54:2, 171:3, 109:4, 117:4, 27:6, 35:6

immoral. *See also* **adultery**
58:1, 69:1, 76:1, 87:1, 171:3, 172:3, 176:4, 88:6

inequality
7:P, 86:1, 114:3, 124:3, 132:3, 139:3, 19:4, 29:4, 36:4, 39:4, 73:4, 85:4, 119:4, 124:4, 125:4, 150:4, 103:5, 38:6, 44:6, 45:6, 78:6

inherit, inheritance
a discussion of the chosen few
63–105:3

Israel
26:P, 18:1, 29:1, 32:1, 36:1, 42:1, 43:1, 45:1, 46:1, 65:1, 100:1, 14:2, 72:2, 81:2, 90:2, 91:2, 94:2, 14:3, 23:3, 31:3, 70:3, 76:3, 77:3, 111:3, 176:3, 180:3, 196:3, 18:4, 73:4, 100:4, 101:4, 104:4, 106:4, 126:4, 130:4, 131:4, 135:4, 150:4, 160:4, 35:5, 36:5, 41:5, 79:5, 110:5, 111:5, 112:5, 113:5, 114:5, 132:5, 4:6, 16:6, 17:6, 20:6, 21:6, 22:6, 46:6, 52:6, 58:6

Index & Concordance   **121**

James E. Faust
  8:P, 83:1, 93:3, 117:3, 43:4, 156:4, 162:4, 45:5, 91:5, 142:5
Jehovah. *See also* **Christ, Jesus**; *See also* **Exemplar**; *See also* **Lamb**; *See also* **Savior**
  18:1, 30:3, 66:4, 98:4, 100:4, 88:5, 98:5, 12:6, 16:6
Jerusalem. *See also* **Salem**
  14:P, 2:1, 9:1, 15:1, 16:1, 33:1, 36:1, 37:1, 47:1, 53:1, 55:1, 61:1, 75:1, 78:1, 104:1, 1:2, 3:2, 51:2, 97:2, 1:3, 9:3, 18:3, 49:3, 100:3, 202:3, 1:4, 41:4, 1:5, 8:5, 20:5, 23:5, 63:5, 73:5, 87:5, 96:5, 97:5, 98:5, 113:5, 117:5, 118:5, 127:5, 128:5, 131:5, 134:5, 1:6
John A. Widtsoe
  8:1, 45:1, 61:1, 72:2, 164:4, 67:5, 93:6
Joseph Fielding Smith
  14:1, 81:1, 15:3, 21:3, 41:3, 56:3, 78:3, 102:3, 103:3, 190:3, 194:3, 208:3, 3:6
Joseph Smith
  4:P, 12:P, 18:P, 33:P, 39:P, 40:P, 41:P, 3:1, 5:1, 15:1, 26:1, 31:1, 32:1, 41:1, 44:1, 46:1, 48:1, 65:1, 67:1, 72:1, 90:1, 94:1, 103:1, 1:2, 3:2, 4:2, 6:2, 10:2, 15:2, 22:2, 23:2, 25:2, 26:2, 27:2, 28:2, 31:2, 42:2, 44:2, 45:2, 50:2, 58:2, 61:2, 62:2, 63:2, 87:2, 88:2, 90:2, 1:3, 5:3, 6:3, 7:3, 12:3, 13:3, 14:3, 15:3, 16:3, 17:3, 18:3, 20:3, 22:3, 25:3, 30:3, 31:3, 36:3, 43:3, 44:3, 57:3, 68:3, 69:3, 77:3, 81:3, 82:3, 83:3, 85:3, 86:3, 87:3, 88:3, 91:3, 93:3, 97:3, 98:3, 99:3, 100:3, 101:3, 104:3, 116:3, 120:3, 122:3, 125:3, 126:3, 140:3, 141:3, 160:3, 166:3, 177:3, 181:3, 182:3, 184:3, 188:3, 190:3, 191:3, 192:3, 193:3, 195:3, 196:3, 198:3, 200:3, 202:3, 203:3, 207:3, 208:3, 1:4, 4:4, 7:4, 10:4, 11:4, 12:4, 13:4, 28:4, 29:4, 30:4, 38:4, 39:4, 44:4, 45:4, 46:4, 48:4, 57:4, 61:4, 65:4, 76:4, 77:4, 78:4, 100:4, 104:4, 107:4, 114:4, 133:4, 137:4, 142:4, 148:4, 157:4, 169:4, 171:4, 1:5, 4:5, 5:5, 8:5, 9:5, 14:5, 20:5, 24:5, 25:5, 27:5, 30:5, 31:5, 33:5, 34:5, 42:5, 45:5, 47:5, 54:5, 55:5, 56:5, 58:5, 64:5, 66:5, 68:5, 77:5, 81:5, 86:5, 88:5, 89:5, 93:5, 94:5, 95:5, 96:5, 97:5, 98:5, 99:5, 100:5, 108:5, 112:5, 118:5, 119:5, 123:5, 124:5, 126:5, 127:5, 129:5, 136:5, 1:6, 3:6, 5:6, 6:6, 16:6, 20:6, 22:6, 25:6, 31:6, 51:6, 56:6, 57:6, 60:6, 87:6, 98:6, 105:6, 106:6, 113:6, 116:6
journey
  a discussion of
    life's journey
      7–57:5
J. Reuben Clark
  44:1, 79:3, 21:4, 28:4
justice, justification
  discussion of
    6–17:2
  rewards those who are obedient to God's laws
    17:2
justified. *See* **justice, justification**
key(s)
  8:P, 23:P, 26:P, 2:1, 13:1, 18:1, 87:1, 101:1, 104:1, 28:2, 61:2, 22:3, 23:3, 24:3, 43:3, 44:3, 57:3, 60:3, 76:3, 83:3, 94:3, 95:3, 97:3, 98:3, 121:3, 122:3, 136:3, 141:3, 156:3,

157:3, 164:3, 176:3, 179:3, 181:3, 184:3, 190:3, 191:3, 192:3, 198:3, 9:4, 62:4, 66:4, 89:4, 106:4, 146:4, 153:4, 159:4, 164:4, 182:4, 26:5, 46:5, 47:5, 54:5, 64:5, 66:5, 87:5, 88:5, 108:5, 134:5, 22:6, 70:6, 94:6, 106:6, 108:6

King Benjamin
20:P, 19:1, 20:1, 21:1, 22:1, 23:1, 24:1, 25:1, 26:1, 8:2, 66:2, 7:3, 8:3, 9:3, 10:3, 11:3, 20:3, 51:3, 67:3, 152:3, 9:4, 35:4, 39:4, 78:4, 120:4, 121:4, 126:4, 127:4, 170:4, 36:5, 42:5, 59:5, 62:5, 63:5, 64:5, 66:5, 106:5, 108:5, 39:6, 46:6, 48:6, 76:6, 79:6, 106:6

king(s)
15:1, 16:1, 20:1, 21:1, 23:1, 25:1, 49:1, 85:2, 90:2, 92:2, 94:2, 95:2, 5:3, 7:3, 9:3, 10:3, 11:3, 29:3, 45:3, 111:3, 112:3, 113:3, 119:3, 139:3, 152:3, 198:3, 199:3, 20:4, 39:4, 76:4, 100:4, 108:4, 134:4, 8:5, 9:5, 39:5, 51:5, 54:5, 58:5, 60:5, 62:5, 63:5, 89:5, 1:6, 2:6, 16:6, 26:6, 46:6, 58:6

Korihor
50:1, 79:1, 127:4, 175:4, 47:6, 88:6

labor. *See also* **work**
35:P, 37:P, 38:P, 42:P, 20:1, 24:1, 27:1, 30:1, 42:1, 84:1, 39:2, 7:3, 19:3, 55:3, 146:3, 171:3, 17:4, 19:4, 39:4, 58:4, 62:4, 70:4, 71:4, 80:4, 82:4, 83:4, 84:4, 85:4, 86:4, 87:4, 88:4, 89:4, 90:4, 91:4, 92:4, 127:4, 135:4, 136:4, 140:4, 141:4, 151:4, 152:4, 156:4, 174:4, 176:4, 183:4, 185:4, 4:5, 26:5, 32:5, 33:5, 50:5, 92:5, 93:5, 95:5, 122:5, 137:5, 48:6, 59:6, 60:6, 65:6, 66:6, 71:6, 72:6, 100:6

lack. *See* **poor**

Laman
101:1, 20:5, 27:5

Lamb. *See also* **Christ, Jesus;** *See also* **Exemplar;** *See also* **Jehovah;** *See also* **Savior**
18:1, 172:4, 98:6

lawyers
86:1, 90:1, 119:4, 103:5, 37:6

Lehi
17:P, 27:P, 63:1, 64:1, 74:1, 94:1, 52:2, 58:2, 78:2, 195:3, 21:4, 42:4, 59:4, 3:5, 8:5, 9:5, 10:5, 17:5, 19:5, 21:5, 23:5, 26:5, 28:5, 31:5, 34:5, 41:5, 42:5, 51:5, 52:5, 58:5, 67:5, 73:5

lies
30:P, 9:1, 18:1, 22:1, 51:1, 63:1, 72:1, 19:2, 97:2, 9:3, 55:3, 60:3, 95:3, 97:3, 117:3, 139:3, 160:3, 181:3, 13:4, 41:4, 47:4, 65:4, 74:4, 137:4, 142:4, 156:4, 166:4, 7:5, 9:5, 19:5, 26:5, 87:5, 2:6, 60:6, 67:6, 101:6, 112:6

Lorenzo Snow
78:1, 6:4, 15:4, 17:4, 31:4, 47:4, 4:5, 94:5, 95:5, 100:5, 131:5, 136:5, 148:5

love. *See also* **charity;** *See also* **heart**
2:P, 7:P, 9:P, 10:P, 11:P, 12:P, 17:P, 20:P, 21:P, 22:P, 24:P, 27:P, 28:P, 34:P, 39:P, 43:P, 19:1, 22:1, 23:1, 24:1, 26:1, 29:1, 30:1, 33:1, 34:1, 42:1, 49:1, 64:1, 65:1, 70:1, 71:1, 76:1, 77:1, 79:1, 86:1, 87:1, 89:1, 91:1, 99:1, 3:2, 4:2, 5:2, 18:2, 19:2, 27:2, 38:2, 41:2, 44:2, 50:2, 54:2, 56:2, 57:2, 60:2, 61:2, 62:2, 66:2, 67:2, 69:2, 70:2,

Index & Concordance

72:2, 73:2, 74:2, 75:2, 76:2, 77:2, 78:2, 79:2, 80:2, 81:2, 82:2, 84:2, 86:2, 93:2, 95:2, 96:2, 97:2, 98:2, 99:2, 17:3, 30:3, 33:3, 44:3, 47:3, 48:3, 49:3, 50:3, 51:3, 52:3, 56:3, 57:3, 61:3, 68:3, 74:3, 75:3, 85:3, 86:3, 87:3, 90:3, 91:3, 92:3, 93:3, 95:3, 104:3, 108:3, 109:3, 111:3, 113:3, 114:3, 117:3, 118:3, 119:3, 122:3, 124:3, 125:3, 131:3, 132:3, 134:3, 138:3, 139:3, 140:3, 141:3, 142:3, 146:3, 147:3, 148:3, 153:3, 154:3, 155:3, 156:3, 157:3, 158:3, 159:3, 168:3, 169:3, 170:3, 171:3, 173:3, 178:3, 182:3, 185:3, 189:3, 203:3, 2:4, 19:4, 21:4, 23:4, 25:4, 26:4, 27:4, 33:4, 34:4, 35:4, 37:4, 38:4, 41:4, 42:4, 47:4, 50:4, 51:4, 52:4, 54:4, 55:4, 56:4, 57:4, 58:4, 60:4, 64:4, 70:4, 72:4, 73:4, 90:4, 91:4, 93:4, 95:4, 97:4, 98:4, 99:4, 100:4, 102:4, 107:4, 114:4, 116:4, 120:4, 121:4, 123:4, 138:4, 141:4, 142:4, 143:4, 146:4, 147:4, 148:4, 149:4, 152:4, 153:4, 155:4, 156:4, 157:4, 158:4, 163:4, 164:4, 165:4, 166:4, 167:4, 168:4, 169:4, 170:4, 171:4, 172:4, 173:4, 174:4, 175:4, 178:4, 179:4, 181:4, 182:4, 183:4, 184:4, 185:4, 186:4, 2:5, 16:5, 24:5, 30:5, 33:5, 42:5, 43:5, 52:5, 64:5, 66:5, 67:5, 69:5, 70:5, 71:5, 74:5, 77:5, 78:5, 79:5, 81:5, 85:5, 89:5, 92:5, 100:5, 106:5, 107:5, 108:5, 122:5, 124:5, 127:5, 133:5, 135:5, 137:5, 2:6, 5:6, 7:6, 8:6, 9:6, 11:6, 13:6, 15:6, 16:6, 18:6, 23:6, 31:6, 35:6, 38:6, 39:6, 43:6, 61:6, 66:6, 67:6, 70:6, 78:6, 79:6, 80:6, 85:6, 86:6, 87:6, 88:6, 91:6, 93:6, 94:6, 95:6, 96:6, 97:6, 98:6, 99:6, 100:6, 101:6, 102:6, 106:6, 107:6, 108:6, 113:6, 116:6, 117:6

low
    to make, is not demeaning
        34:4

Lucifer. *See also* **adversary;** *See also* **devil;** *See also* **hell;** *See also* **Satan**
    10:1

lukewarm
    being, is a one-way ticket to hell
        47:1

Mahan
    51:1, 52:1, 69:1, 79:1, 127:4, 151:4, 47:6

mammon. *See also* **materialism;** *See also* **money;** *See also* **riches**
    a discussion of
        choosing, over God
            99–137:4
    making friends with
        109:4

mansions
    37:P, 76:1, 73:2, 82:2, 86:2, 89:2, 93:2, 168:3, 203:3, 81:4, 175:4, 50:5, 100:6

marriage. *See also* **new and everlasting covenant**
    a discussion of
        how it's likened to new and everlasting covenant
            72–99:2

martyrdom
    34:1, 58:2

materialism. *See also* **mammon**
    25:P, 41:P, 62:1, 64:1, 68:1, 102:1, 109:4, 93:5, 26:6, 76:6

Matthew Cowley
    3:P, 4:P, 6:1, 46:1, 105:6

Melchizedek
    administered priesthood to Abraham/built temple in Salem
        16:1

Melchizedek Priesthood. *See also* **Aaronic Priesthood;** *See also* **oath and covenant of the priesthood;** *See also* **patriarchal order of the priesthood;** *See also* **priesthood**
    a discussion of
        4–209:3

merchandise. *See* **mammon;** *See* **money**

mercy. *See also* **grace**
    10:P, 17:P, 20:P, 21:P, 22:P, 23:P, 24:P, 23:1, 26:1, 30:1, 66:1, 100:1, 4:2, 6:2, 7:2, 8:2, 9:2, 10:2, 15:2, 16:2, 17:2, 18:2, 20:2, 23:2, 24:2, 26:2, 27:2, 28:2, 29:2, 30:2, 32:2, 34:2, 35:2, 36:2, 45:2, 57:2, 97:2, 54:3, 71:3, 156:3, 159:3, 165:3, 167:3, 98:4, 112:4, 122:4, 129:4, 130:4, 143:4, 148:4, 151:4, 179:4, 15:5, 16:5, 19:5, 44:5, 64:5, 77:5, 106:5, 113:5, 114:5, 124:5, 12:6, 29:6, 41:6, 49:6, 51:6, 82:6, 102:6

miracle
    17:P, 25:1, 30:1, 66:1, 64:2, 155:3, 9:4, 36:4, 51:4, 57:4, 60:4, 67:4, 70:4, 159:4, 160:4, 162:4, 163:4, 173:4, 25:5, 32:5, 39:5, 66:5, 101:5, 109:5, 99:6

miserable
    49:1, 50:1, 51:1, 60:1, 77:1, 78:1, 8:2, 16:2, 89:2, 132:3, 63:4, 13:5, 14:5, 16:5, 56:5, 30:6

money. *See also* **mammon;** *See also* **materialism;** *See also* **riches**
    love of, is root of all evil
        70:1

Moroni
    1:1, 31:1, 61:1, 90:1, 91:1, 92:1, 103:1, 12:3, 65:3, 68:3, 92:3, 166:3, 195:3, 209:3, 210:3, 5:4, 6:4, 107:4, 123:4, 124:4, 149:4, 165:4, 166:4, 174:4, 175:4, 178:4, 181:4, 182:4, 183:4, 31:5, 44:5, 53:5, 55:5, 70:5, 77:5, 109:5, 112:5, 118:5, 119:5, 22:6, 23:6, 43:6, 86:6, 100:6

mortality
    is testing ground for our genuine desires
        47:1

Moses
    4:P, 26:P, 18:1, 19:1, 28:1, 32:1, 34:1, 51:1, 74:1, 87:1, 88:1, 8:2, 22:2, 40:2, 81:2, 84:2, 14:3, 15:3, 16:3, 17:3, 18:3, 20:3, 23:3, 24:3, 40:3, 55:3, 63:3, 65:3, 66:3, 76:3, 77:3, 88:3, 89:3, 99:3, 104:3, 110:3, 175:3, 176:3, 177:3, 184:3, 195:3, 207:3, 208:3, 47:4, 50:4, 100:4, 101:4, 112:4, 118:4, 120:4, 126:4, 129:4, 151:4, 165:4, 166:4, 8:5, 9:5, 18:5, 23:5, 31:5, 32:5, 35:5, 41:5, 42:5, 54:5, 55:5, 67:5, 72:5, 74:5, 79:5, 86:5, 89:5, 112:5, 131:5, 16:6, 17:6, 29:6, 36:6, 38:6, 46:6, 49:6, 50:6, 94:6, 95:6

Index & Concordance

mother
> 46:1, 61:1, 62:1, 25:2, 51:2, 85:2, 59:3, 126:3, 158:3, 28:4, 110:4, 172:4, 21:5, 129:5, 27:6, 52:6, 98:6, 106:6, 109:6

murder
> 50:1, 53:1, 60:1, 62:1, 63:1, 69:1, 80:1, 90:1, 102:1, 96:2, 119:3, 146:3, 160:3, 53:4, 118:4, 137:4, 14:5, 108:5, 36:6, 60:6

murmur
> 22:2, 26:5

mysteries
> 26:P, 32:P, 39:P, 40:P, 18:1, 61:1, 44:2, 8:3, 10:3, 24:3, 30:3, 31:3, 43:3, 47:3, 49:3, 57:3, 72:3, 81:3, 87:3, 93:3, 95:3, 96:3, 97:3, 98:3, 176:3, 177:3, 181:3, 183:3, 187:3, 188:3, 189:3, 190:3, 191:3, 192:3, 46:4, 100:4, 108:4, 149:4, 59:5, 60:5, 66:5, 79:5, 85:5, 86:5, 87:5, 88:5, 116:5, 119:5, 16:6, 25:6, 115:6

natural man
> 25:P, 22:1, 78:1, 20:2, 21:2, 50:2, 178:3, 64:4, 95:4, 169:4, 182:4, 23:5, 25:5, 42:5, 43:5, 44:5, 45:5, 68:5, 76:5, 84:5, 91:5, 9:6, 86:6

Neal A. Maxwell
> 12:1, 40:1, 110:3, 118:3, 148:3, 15:4, 27:4, 57:4, 79:4, 148:5

needy. *See also* **poor**
> 3:1, 20:1, 24:1, 27:1, 56:1, 80:1, 91:1, 48:3, 114:3, 129:3, 7:4, 11:4, 14:4, 23:4, 24:4, 29:4, 33:4, 40:4, 54:4, 72:4, 75:4, 82:4, 90:4, 107:4, 117:4, 121:4, 122:4, 123:4, 124:4, 125:4, 126:4, 129:4, 130:4, 133:4, 139:4, 144:4, 149:4, 153:4, 158:4, 170:4, 179:4, 180:4, 71:5, 5:6, 8:6, 23:6, 36:6, 41:6, 43:6, 44:6, 45:6, 46:6, 50:6, 52:6, 56:6, 63:6, 67:6, 72:6, 76:6, 87:6, 95:6, 104:6, 105:6, 106:6, 107:6, 109:6, 113:6

Nehor
> 26:1, 84:1, 145:3

neighbor
> 7:P, 8:P, 9:P, 28:P, 30:P, 19:1, 29:1, 66:1, 18:3, 49:3, 96:3, 182:3, 21:4, 26:4, 33:4, 38:4, 56:4, 58:4, 77:4, 91:4, 100:4, 104:4, 118:4, 122:4, 158:4, 164:4, 165:4, 169:4, 184:4, 93:5, 94:5, 127:5, 16:6, 20:6, 36:6, 41:6, 77:6, 93:6, 94:6, 113:6

new and everlasting covenant. *See also* **marriage**
> a discussion of
>> how it's likened to marriage
>>> 72–99:2

Nimrod
> 51:1, 52:1, 53:1, 54:1, 55:1, 58:1, 61:1, 101:1

Noah
> 15:P, 14:1, 15:1, 16:1, 18:1, 36:1, 53:1, 55:1, 86:1, 87:1, 101:1, 102:1, 103:1, 7:3, 27:3, 207:3, 107:4, 32:5, 88:5, 101:5, 124:5, 125:5, 127:5, 22:6

oath and covenant of the priesthood. *See also* **priesthood**
> 1:P, 6:1, 32:1, 9:2, 34:2, 36:2, 47:2, 61:2, 98:2, 1:3, 2:3, 3:3, 4:3, 6:3, 21:3, 25:3, 30:3, 33:3, 35:3, 36:3, 39:3, 40:3, 41:3, 43:3, 47:3, 49:3, 53:3, 54:3, 55:3, 58:3, 59:3, 60:3, 61:3, 63:3,

64:3, 66:3, 68:3, 71:3, 72:3, 76:3, 77:3, 78:3, 80:3, 81:3, 82:3, 85:3, 87:3, 88:3, 90:3, 93:3, 94:3, 95:3, 97:3, 98:3, 102:3, 103:3, 104:3, 105:3, 106:3, 109:3, 115:3, 117:3, 126:3, 131:3, 135:3, 139:3, 140:3, 142:3, 143:3, 144:3, 159:3, 172:3, 173:3, 174:3, 175:3, 177:3, 179:3, 184:3, 189:3, 190:3, 193:3, 202:3, 208:3, 210:3, 211:3, 212:3, 213:3, 214:3, 1:4, 2:4, 14:4, 72:4, 90:4, 129:4, 142:4, 185:4, 1:5, 2:5, 59:5, 116:5, 134:5, 135:5, 136:5, 50:6

obedience
30:P, 32:P, 41:P, 17:1, 19:1, 21:1, 48:1, 3:2, 4:2, 6:2, 7:2, 10:2, 12:2, 13:2, 15:2, 17:2, 28:2, 29:2, 33:2, 34:2, 35:2, 37:2, 38:2, 39:2, 42:2, 51:2, 61:2, 31:3, 67:3, 68:3, 71:3, 75:3, 80:3, 94:3, 118:3, 121:3, 124:3, 126:3, 131:3, 134:3, 135:3, 146:3, 203:3, 208:3, 212:3, 16:4, 18:4, 26:4, 36:4, 41:4, 45:4, 50:4, 56:4, 60:4, 65:4, 67:4, 102:4, 156:4, 180:4, 7:5, 33:5, 35:5, 36:5, 45:5, 46:5, 47:5, 81:5, 84:5, 97:5, 135:5, 18:6, 112:6, 113:6, 115:6

offence
73:1

offering. *See* consecration; sacrifice; *See* offerings

offerings
those, ordered by Satan are always rejected by God
51:1

oneness. *See also* unity
6:P, 18:P, 19:P, 12:1, 49:1, 92:1, 23:2, 24:2, 25:2, 27:2, 28:2, 29:2, 48:2, 71:2, 79:2, 170:3, 5:4, 18:4, 31:4, 41:4, 42:4, 43:4, 44:4, 45:4, 47:4, 59:4, 65:5, 94:5, 115:5, 123:5

opposition. *See also* adversity
35:P, 33:1, 36:1, 54:1, 67:1, 70:1, 19:2, 26:2, 56:2, 117:3, 45:4, 62:4, 10:5, 18:5, 49:5

ordinance
6:1, 11:1, 31:1, 51:1, 28:2, 31:2, 34:2, 36:2, 37:2, 38:2, 45:2, 53:2, 56:2, 63:2, 64:2, 67:2, 69:2, 91:2, 4:3, 6:3, 9:3, 10:3, 14:3, 16:3, 20:3, 21:3, 28:3, 29:3, 77:3, 82:3, 84:3, 87:3, 99:3, 105:3, 194:3, 197:3, 205:3, 212:3, 28:4, 43:4, 159:4, 160:4, 161:4, 162:4, 163:4, 25:5, 46:5, 60:5, 91:5, 133:5, 75:6

parent
42:1, 46:1, 168:3, 53:4, 147:4, 153:4, 16:5, 62:5, 70:6

patience
23:1, 27:1, 73:1, 22:2, 76:2, 85:2, 86:2, 29:3, 97:3, 129:3, 148:3, 149:3, 150:3, 151:3, 155:3, 178:3, 181:3, 99:4, 146:4, 155:4, 178:4, 184:4, 85:5, 15:6, 70:6, 101:6

patriarchal order of the priesthood. *See also* **Melchizedek Priesthood**; *See also* oath and covenant of the priesthood

Paul
27:P, 39:P, 41:1, 57:1, 59:1, 70:1, 73:1, 88:1, 89:1, 91:1, 103:1, 27:2, 63:2, 64:2, 81:2, 85:2, 31:3, 40:3, 67:3, 90:3, 100:3, 149:3, 163:3, 171:3, 180:3, 189:3, 198:3, 37:4, 99:4, 117:4, 165:4, 166:4, 184:4, 13:5, 15:5, 29:5, 89:5, 119:5, 133:5, 15:6, 35:6, 76:6, 78:6, 94:6, 95:6, 97:6, 106:6

Paymaster
8:P, 17:1, 151:3, 70:4, 71:4, 88:4, 90:4, 183:4

Index & Concordance

peace
> 2:P, 5:P, 8:P, 12:P, 17:P, 20:P, 26:P, 27:P, 9:1, 15:1, 16:1, 23:1, 25:1, 27:1, 30:1, 46:1, 88:1, 8:2, 24:2, 39:2, 50:2, 51:2, 61:2, 95:2, 5:3, 6:3, 7:3, 8:3, 18:3, 28:3, 29:3, 46:3, 50:3, 66:3, 70:3, 83:3, 114:3, 119:3, 129:3, 140:3, 167:3, 172:3, 173:3, 199:3, 19:4, 22:4, 40:4, 44:4, 46:4, 115:4, 118:4, 119:4, 124:4, 125:4, 137:4, 140:4, 150:4, 151:4, 152:4, 162:4, 171:4, 172:4, 178:4, 27:5, 28:5, 38:5, 44:5, 46:5, 53:5, 55:5, 81:5, 83:5, 92:5, 94:5, 103:5, 104:5, 106:5, 107:5, 122:5, 128:5, 130:5, 132:5, 133:5, 1:6, 2:6, 13:6, 34:6, 37:6, 38:6, 45:6, 60:6, 61:6, 64:6, 97:6, 98:6, 101:6

persecute
> 27:P, 28:P, 30:P, 61:1, 67:1, 85:1, 91:1, 137:3, 152:3, 108:4, 122:4, 123:4, 124:4, 150:4, 42:5, 26:6, 41:6, 42:6, 44:6, 77:6, 112:6, 113:6

plague
> 82:1, 160:3, 124:4, 38:5, 44:6

poor. *See also* **needy**
>> a discussion of
>>> how we treat the,
>>>> 120–137:4

popular
> 14:1, 66:1, 81:1, 83:1, 84:1, 87:1, 25:3, 132:3

possession. *See* **mammon**

praise. *See* **popular**

pray, prayer
> 80:1, 85:1, 98:1, 14:2, 20:2, 55:2, 86:2, 91:2, 92:2, 41:3, 70:3, 154:3, 158:3, 192:3, 197:3, 8:4, 9:4, 45:4, 46:4, 54:4, 60:4, 111:4, 112:4, 140:4, 162:4, 163:4, 181:4, 4:5, 19:5, 42:5, 51:5, 53:5, 67:5, 69:5, 77:5, 78:5, 87:5, 112:5, 114:5, 115:5, 116:5, 120:5, 121:5, 122:5, 123:5, 124:5, 28:6, 29:6, 64:6, 90:6, 104:6

premortal existence
>> mature knowledge of gospel from, planted deep in our souls
>>> 44:1

pride
>> neither rich nor poor exempt from
>>> 24:1

priest
> 17:1, 26:1, 84:1, 20:2, 41:2, 94:2, 95:2, 5:3, 6:3, 7:3, 9:3, 29:3, 42:3, 46:3, 65:3, 119:3, 152:3, 190:3, 198:3, 199:3, 88:4, 100:4, 40:5, 63:5, 89:5, 16:6

priestcraft
> 26:1, 51:1, 53:1, 61:1, 68:1, 84:1, 85:1, 145:3, 146:3

priesthood. *See also* **Aaronic Priesthood**; *See also* **Melchizedek Priesthood**; *See also* **oath and covenant of the priesthood**; *See also* **patriarchal order of the priesthood**
>> a discussion of
>>> Melchizedek
>>>> 4–11:3, 182–192:3, 204–210:3

oath and covenant of the
- 39–60:3

restoration of the
- 12–16:3

priesthood society
- 1:P, 3:P, 4:P, 43:P, 3:1, 5:1, 6:1, 7:1, 12:1, 14:1, 46:1, 5:3, 6:3, 12:3, 21:3, 25:3, 28:3, 32:3, 35:3, 61:3, 85:3, 127:3, 206:3, 7:4, 14:4, 15:4, 22:4, 31:4, 74:4, 80:4, 90:5, 98:5, 99:5, 127:5, 87:6, 102:6, 105:6

princess. *See* **queen**

prison
- 88:1, 51:2, 52:2, 54:2, 88:2, 70:3, 100:3, 138:4, 139:4, 151:4, 152:4, 12:5, 29:5, 39:5, 75:5, 63:6, 116:6, 117:6

probation. *See* **mortality**

progress

perspective of our, compared to steps on an airplane
- 90:5

properties. *See* **property**

property

converting life into, is Satan's great secret
- 47:6

prophecies
- 93:1, 95:1, 97:1, 98:1, 109:3, 166:3, 4:5, 97:5, 103:5, 118:5, 119:5, 49:6

prosper. *See* **abundance**

publicans
- 80:1

pure in heart. *See also* **Zion**
- 2:P, 17:P, 25:P, 26:P, 38:P, 41:P, 43:P, 2:1, 3:1, 4:1, 6:1, 8:1, 12:1, 15:1, 19:1, 25:1, 33:1, 46:1, 48:1, 18:2, 47:3, 66:3, 71:3, 87:3, 161:3, 172:3, 178:3, 195:3, 207:3, 208:3, 2:4, 15:4, 16:4, 31:4, 73:4, 83:4, 95:4, 104:4, 109:4, 147:4, 1:5, 2:5, 3:5, 4:5, 18:5, 77:5, 78:5, 79:5, 80:5, 81:5, 82:5, 84:5, 87:5, 89:5, 90:5, 91:5, 93:5, 94:5, 95:5, 96:5, 101:5, 109:5, 114:5, 115:5, 116:5, 117:5, 118:5, 119:5, 120:5, 124:5, 125:5, 127:5, 130:5, 133:5, 134:5, 136:5, 9:6, 20:6, 26:6, 75:6, 76:6, 78:6, 116:6

purification
- 14:P, 18:2, 19:2, 20:2, 90:2, 91:2, 66:3, 137:3, 52:4, 162:4, 182:4, 3:5, 25:5, 26:5, 75:5, 79:5, 90:5, 115:5, 116:5, 120:5

queen(s)
- 93:1, 90:2, 93:2, 94:2, 199:3, 8:5

rainbow

sign of everlasting covenant
- 15:1

redeem, Redeemer, redemption

noble spirits in premortal life carried out work of
- 45:1

Index & Concordance

repent
20:P, 2:1, 10:1, 13:1, 16:1, 24:1, 70:1, 91:1, 98:1, 99:1, 5:2, 7:2, 16:2, 17:2, 19:2, 35:2, 36:2, 96:2, 5:3, 6:3, 19:3, 45:3, 46:3, 70:3, 103:3, 135:3, 153:3, 161:3, 188:3, 205:3, 37:4, 69:4, 84:4, 102:4, 111:4, 112:4, 117:4, 118:4, 121:4, 126:4, 135:4, 136:4, 148:4, 15:5, 46:5, 78:5, 82:5, 105:5, 106:5, 109:5, 2:6, 18:6, 28:6, 29:6, 35:6, 36:6, 39:6, 46:6, 47:6, 59:6, 60:6

resurrected
14:P, 13:1, 28:1, 64:1, 86:1, 95:1, 14:2, 26:2, 17:3, 91:3, 202:3, 203:3, 42:4, 13:5, 64:5, 105:5, 108:5, 121:5, 122:5, 132:5

revelation
    is key to magnifying callings and to learning
        95:3

riches. *See also* **mammon;** *See also* **materialism;** *See also* **money;** *See also* **wealth**
30:P, 32:P, 34:P, 38:P, 17:1, 27:1, 31:1, 33:1, 67:1, 71:1, 72:1, 76:1, 84:1, 86:1, 92:1, 93:1, 95:1, 96:1, 97:1, 99:1, 123:3, 125:3, 126:3, 128:3, 129:3, 130:3, 131:3, 133:3, 141:3, 142:3, 146:3, 167:3, 171:3, 193:3, 8:4, 9:4, 10:4, 26:4, 30:4, 38:4, 40:4, 69:4, 72:4, 83:4, 84:4, 85:4, 87:4, 88:4, 91:4, 93:4, 95:4, 99:4, 100:4, 101:4, 102:4, 103:4, 106:4, 108:4, 109:4, 110:4, 111:4, 113:4, 115:4, 116:4, 117:4, 118:4, 119:4, 120:4, 123:4, 124:4, 126:4, 127:4, 130:4, 132:4, 133:4, 135:4, 140:4, 142:4, 144:4, 148:4, 149:4, 150:4, 152:4, 158:4, 184:4, 44:5, 103:5, 104:5, 4:6, 7:6, 16:6, 17:6, 18:6, 19:6, 22:6, 25:6, 26:6, 28:6, 31:6, 33:6, 34:6, 36:6, 37:6, 38:6, 43:6, 44:6, 46:6, 47:6, 48:6, 51:6, 56:6, 57:6, 58:6, 65:6, 67:6, 72:6, 113:6, 114:6, 115:6

Sabbath
42:P, 37:1, 38:2, 39:2, 40:2, 50:2, 51:2, 72:2, 99:4, 53:5, 15:6

sacrament
14:P, 23:P, 29:1, 14:2, 20:2, 36:2, 38:2, 39:2, 40:2, 41:2, 60:2, 67:2, 80:2, 81:2, 82:2, 89:2, 9:3, 11:3, 39:3, 42:3, 66:3, 75:3, 93:3, 165:3, 193:3, 210:3, 46:4, 17:5, 18:5, 60:5, 61:5, 62:5, 64:5, 117:5, 121:5

sacrifice. *See also* **consecration;** *See also* **offering**
    a discussion of
        3–31:4, 33–52:4, 61–92:4

Salem. *See also* **Jerusalem**
3:P, 9:1, 15:1, 16:1, 5:3, 27:3, 29:3, 45:3, 1:6, 2:6

salvation, plan of
50:1, 54:2, 25:3, 26:3, 31:3, 36:3, 68:3, 73:3, 12:5, 126:5, 130:5

sanctification
14:P, 18:P, 18:2, 20:2, 21:2, 90:2, 91:2, 9:3, 56:3, 66:3, 67:3, 68:3, 69:3, 70:3, 71:3, 74:3, 75:3, 77:3, 84:3, 104:3, 137:3, 210:3, 14:4, 18:4, 21:4, 31:4, 52:4, 182:4, 3:5, 27:5, 47:5, 75:5, 79:5, 90:5, 94:5, 99:5, 115:5, 116:5

sanctified body. *See* **sanctification**

sanctuaries. *See* **mammon**

Satan. *See also* **adversary**; *See also* **devil**; *See also* **hell**; *See also* **Lucifer**
    we must understand, in order to confront him
        55:5
savior
    Adam empowered to become, to his family
        11:1
Savior. *See* **Christ, Jesus**; *See* **Exemplar**; *See* **Jehovah**; *See* **Lamb**
saviors on Mount Zion
    43:1, 32:2, 40:2, 25:3, 35:3, 37:3, 43:3, 66:3, 69:3, 104:3, 156:3, 144:4, 184:4, 64:5, 116:5, 68:6
science
    57:1, 81:1, 83:1, 14:2, 163:3
seal
    26:1, 24:2, 76:2, 79:2, 93:2, 13:3, 16:3, 17:3, 81:3, 84:3, 99:3, 149:3, 168:3, 194:3, 199:3, 209:3, 52:4, 75:4, 108:4, 155:4, 162:4, 38:5, 58:5, 65:5, 67:5, 25:6
secret combinations. *See also* **Gadianton robbers**
    49:1, 60:1, 61:1, 91:1, 97:1, 99:1, 102:5, 103:5, 108:5
selfish
    9:P, 38:P, 58:1, 73:1, 89:1, 91:1, 96:1, 19:2, 32:2, 71:2, 21:3, 74:3, 88:3, 122:3, 124:3, 125:3, 131:3, 137:3, 153:3, 154:3, 157:3, 171:3, 27:4, 55:4, 82:4, 91:4, 97:4, 98:4, 112:4, 117:4, 134:4, 140:4, 141:4, 145:4, 149:4, 152:4, 156:4, 165:4, 169:4, 176:4, 94:5, 11:6, 18:6, 29:6, 30:6, 31:6, 35:6, 37:6, 45:6, 48:6, 58:6, 64:6, 65:6, 66:6, 68:6, 71:6, 72:6, 77:6, 86:6, 88:6, 94:6, 108:6, 115:6
selfless. *See also* **charity**
    1:P, 8:P, 10:P, 12:P, 23:P, 25:P, 31:P, 24:1, 29:1, 5:2, 32:2, 71:2, 21:3, 51:3, 171:3, 109:4, 170:4, 93:5, 100:5, 26:6, 76:6, 87:6
Sermon on the Mount. *See also* **Beatitudes**
    14:P, 16:P, 28:1, 18:2, 82:5, 118:5
servant
    37:P, 16:1, 27:1, 34:2, 61:2, 62:2, 69:2, 87:2, 88:2, 91:2, 92:2, 96:2, 6:3, 30:3, 41:3, 72:3, 82:3, 100:3, 101:3, 103:3, 115:3, 196:3, 211:3, 214:3, 12:4, 49:4, 50:4, 53:4, 74:4, 75:4, 78:4, 79:4, 81:4, 89:4, 183:4, 66:5, 97:5, 110:5
set apart. *See* **consecration**
sex
    57:1, 66:1, 76:1, 154:3, 97:4, 11:6
single women
    64:3
slippery treasures
    110:4, 27:6
snare
    70:1, 73:1, 109:3, 122:3, 124:3, 139:3, 99:4, 103:4, 113:4, 14:5, 15:6, 19:6, 30:6, 108:6

Index & Concordance

Sodom
> 1:1, 54:1, 55:1, 56:1, 57:1, 86:1, 94:1, 101:1, 102:1, 103:1, 5:4, 121:4, 23:5, 41:6

sorrow. *See also* **wailing**
> 21:P, 34:1, 35:1, 63:1, 93:1, 102:1, 88:2, 51:3, 151:3, 160:3, 19:4, 124:4, 127:4, 136:4, 10:5, 43:5, 44:5, 106:5, 44:6, 48:6, 59:6, 79:6

soul
> 11:P, 16:P, 17:P, 23:P, 43:P, 20:1, 21:1, 22:1, 28:1, 60:1, 76:1, 8:2, 19:2, 26:2, 40:2, 41:2, 49:2, 55:2, 59:2, 61:2, 94:2, 7:3, 19:3, 44:3, 47:3, 67:3, 69:3, 83:3, 97:3, 100:3, 102:3, 108:3, 116:3, 119:3, 122:3, 144:3, 151:3, 156:3, 159:3, 165:3, 166:3, 172:3, 175:3, 182:3, 184:3, 189:3, 193:3, 213:3, 2:4, 9:4, 16:4, 20:4, 50:4, 54:4, 56:4, 60:4, 64:4, 65:4, 111:4, 114:4, 115:4, 118:4, 127:4, 140:4, 146:4, 152:4, 155:4, 160:4, 162:4, 164:4, 166:4, 167:4, 171:4, 172:4, 174:4, 175:4, 179:4, 180:4, 182:4, 183:4, 186:4, 2:5, 13:5, 15:5, 17:5, 44:5, 45:5, 49:5, 68:5, 71:5, 74:5, 80:5, 81:5, 84:5, 100:5, 108:5, 122:5, 5:6, 6:6, 29:6, 30:6, 32:6, 33:6, 37:6, 48:6, 50:6, 65:6, 71:6, 85:6, 86:6, 91:6, 95:6, 96:6, 97:6, 98:6, 100:6, 101:6, 102:6, 103:6, 108:6

Spencer W. Kimball
> 8:P, 25:P, 33:P, 3:1, 7:1, 37:1, 55:1, 85:1, 21:3, 31:3, 35:3, 118:3, 140:3, 191:3, 7:4, 9:4, 15:4, 17:4, 23:4, 30:4, 31:4, 48:4, 59:4, 83:4, 86:4, 109:4, 134:4, 172:4, 173:4, 177:4, 37:5, 49:5, 92:5, 93:5, 98:5, 100:5, 26:6, 57:6, 76:6, 88:6, 90:6, 98:6, 99:6

stewardship(s)
> in heaven based on stewardships on earth
>> 50:5

storehouse
> 7:P, 36:P, 17:1, 18:1, 64:2, 6:3, 38:4, 39:4, 48:4, 61:4, 71:4, 72:4, 74:4, 75:4, 77:4, 79:4, 83:4, 88:4, 91:4, 96:4, 131:4, 10:6, 51:6, 77:6

submission
> 79:1, 118:3, 152:3, 31:5

surplus
> 36:P, 18:1, 48:3, 12:4, 24:4, 69:4, 74:4, 75:4, 79:4, 90:4, 91:4, 94:4, 147:4, 9:6, 114:6

telestial
> 3:P, 9:P, 10:P, 12:P, 25:P, 26:P, 30:P, 31:P, 32:P, 37:P, 38:P, 3:1, 6:1, 7:1, 8:1, 10:1, 17:1, 29:1, 39:1, 40:1, 47:1, 66:1, 80:1, 103:1, 14:2, 15:2, 23:2, 48:2, 60:2, 68:2, 69:2, 68:3, 80:3, 89:3, 114:3, 117:3, 124:3, 125:3, 140:3, 141:3, 144:3, 164:3, 211:3, 10:4, 15:4, 18:4, 25:4, 34:4, 35:4, 36:4, 64:4, 69:4, 73:4, 82:4, 83:4, 96:4, 101:4, 105:4, 141:4, 147:4, 148:4, 163:4, 185:4, 11:5, 12:5, 19:5, 31:5, 36:5, 70:5, 76:5, 84:5, 85:5, 91:5, 121:5, 126:5, 10:6, 17:6, 21:6, 66:6, 86:6, 105:6, 106:6, 107:6, 110:6, 112:6, 115:6, 116:6

temple
> covenants, necessary to establish Zion/is gathering place for Zion people
>> 31:1

temptation
> 70:1, 133:3, 176:3, 43:4, 97:4, 99:4, 14:5, 120:5, 121:5, 11:6, 15:6

Ten Commandments
    15:2, 100:4, 148:4, 110:5, 16:6

ten virgins
    85:1, 103:1, 87:2, 90:2, 92:2

terrestrial
    testimony, bearing of, purifies heart; bearing of, is an act of love
        56:3

tithes
    31:P, 34:P, 37:P, 42:P, 17:1, 37:1, 6:3, 8:4, 12:4, 13:4, 30:4, 81:4, 88:4, 89:4, 92:4, 96:4, 147:4, 118:5, 10:6, 12:6, 13:6, 51:6, 114:6, 115:6

tradition
    98:1, 72:2, 73:2, 75:2, 84:2, 7:3, 9:3

treasure. *See* **mammon**

trial(s). *See also* **adversity**; *See also* **opposition**
    29:P, 44:1, 56:2, 58:2, 83:3, 128:3, 148:3, 151:3, 124:4, 23:5, 27:5, 50:5, 58:5, 44:6, 50:6

unite, unity. *See also* **oneness**
    4:P, 6:P, 37:P, 3:1, 9:1, 14:1, 19:1, 68:1, 77:1, 78:1, 92:1, 23:2, 24:2, 25:2, 27:2, 69:2, 93:2, 74:3, 85:3, 114:3, 116:3, 140:3, 147:3, 170:3, 2:4, 19:4, 33:4, 41:4, 42:4, 43:4, 44:4, 45:4, 46:4, 47:4, 48:4, 49:4, 50:4, 51:4, 52:4, 54:4, 55:4, 58:4, 59:4, 60:4, 62:4, 82:4, 156:4, 171:4, 183:4, 185:4, 2:5, 50:5, 73:5, 100:5, 108:5, 97:6

universe
    composition of
        89:3

vain
    22:P, 28:P, 64:1, 66:1, 69:1, 80:1, 86:1, 97:1, 98:1, 41:2, 45:3, 47:3, 51:3, 92:3, 107:3, 110:3, 114:3, 119:3, 135:3, 146:3, 153:3, 163:3, 164:3, 99:4, 110:4, 111:4, 115:4, 117:4, 118:4, 119:4, 122:4, 124:4, 126:4, 127:4, 133:4, 149:4, 175:4, 181:4, 57:5, 71:5, 95:5, 101:5, 102:5, 104:5, 4:6, 15:6, 28:6, 33:6, 36:6, 38:6, 41:6, 42:6, 44:6, 46:6, 57:6, 79:6, 104:6

veil
    40:1, 55:1, 80:2, 83:2, 84:2, 85:2, 95:2, 26:3, 91:3, 102:3, 178:3, 179:3, 180:3, 181:3, 183:3, 196:3, 209:3, 210:3, 54:4, 12:5, 67:5, 68:5, 79:5, 85:5, 89:5, 109:5, 131:5

violence
    14:1, 36:1, 87:1, 93:1, 95:1, 8:3, 121:3, 108:4, 26:6

wailing. *See also* **sorrow**
    94:1

war
    17:P, 26:P, 42:1, 44:1, 55:1, 62:1, 69:1, 78:1, 80:1, 85:1, 91:1, 102:1, 28:2, 83:3, 108:4, 137:4, 37:5, 102:5, 103:5, 108:5, 26:6, 60:6

warn
    95:1, 113:4, 124:4, 102:5, 103:5, 30:6, 44:6

Index & Concordance

wealth. *See also* **mammon;** *See also* **poor;** *See also* **riches**
    a discussion of
        proper use
            120–151:4
        seeking
            99–137:4

weapon
    29:P, 57:1, 71:1, 55:2, 99:4, 109:4, 132:4, 149:4, 16:6, 26:6, 56:6, 112:6

whore. *See* **Babylon**

wickedness
    today's level of, equals or exceeds times that of Noah's generation
        87:1

widow
    93:1, 7:4, 29:4, 104:4, 109:4, 130:4, 140:4, 146:4, 153:4, 51:5, 70:5, 20:6, 27:6, 52:6, 65:6, 70:6

wife. *See also* **marriage**
    45:P, 10:1, 33:1, 62:1, 24:2, 25:2, 58:2, 66:2, 74:2, 76:2, 77:2, 78:2, 79:2, 85:2, 92:2, 94:2, 95:2, 97:2, 13:3, 15:3, 17:3, 23:3, 31:3, 59:3, 82:3, 85:3, 110:3, 112:3, 126:3, 136:3, 183:3, 198:3, 199:3, 207:3, 211:3, 26:4, 41:4, 43:4, 45:4, 52:4, 98:4, 100:4, 156:4, 157:4, 10:5, 20:5, 24:5, 38:5, 42:5, 11:6, 16:6, 106:6, 109:6

wilderness. *See also* **Babylon**
    a discussion of
        our journey through the
            12–41:5

Wilford Woodruff
    40:1, 55:3, 131:3, 211:3, 148:5

wisdom
    21:P, 32:P, 23:1, 24:1, 26:1, 31:1, 33:1, 39:1, 59:1, 60:1, 64:1, 65:1, 78:1, 84:1, 98:1, 102:1, 45:2, 50:3, 54:3, 71:3, 93:3, 152:3, 161:3, 163:3, 164:3, 165:3, 166:3, 167:3, 168:3, 187:3, 201:3, 208:3, 6:4, 26:4, 27:4, 66:4, 77:4, 100:4, 105:4, 108:4, 109:4, 120:4, 122:4, 137:4, 141:4, 149:4, 152:4, 179:4, 65:5, 3:6, 16:6, 21:6, 25:6, 27:6, 38:6, 42:6, 61:6, 66:6, 82:6, 102:6, 115:6

work. *See also* **labor**
    Christ's, takes priority
        30:1

world, worldly. *See also* **Babylon**
    in, but not of
        74:1

yoke
    17:P, 23:P, 28:P, 62:1, 63:1, 101:1, 92:2, 160:3, 179:4, 68:5, 69:5, 71:5, 102:6

Zion
    an individual with a pure heart
        12:1
    begins in each person's heart
        1:1, 12:1, 13:1
    definition of, is perfection
        12:1
    is a return to the presence of God
        47:1
    is our ideal
        6:1
    principles of
        19:1
    we are
        46:1

Zion people
    characteristics of
        12:1
    temple gathering place for
        14:1

Index & Concordance

About the Author

Larry Barkdull is a longtime publisher and writer of books, music, art, and magazines. For nine years, he owned Sonos Music Resources and published the Tabernacle Choir Performance Library. He was also the owner and publisher of Keepsake Books. Over the past thirty years, he published some six hundred products for numerous authors, composers, and artists. He founded two nonprofit organizations: The Latter-day Foundation for the Arts, Education and Humanity (to promote LDS arts), and Gospel Ideals International (to promote the gospel of Jesus Christ on the Internet).

His books have sold in excess of 300,000 copies, and they have been translated into Japanese, Korean, Italian, and Hebrew. He is the recipient of the American Family Literary Award; the Benjamin Franklin Book Award; and *Foreword Magazine's* GOLD Book of the Year Award for best fiction. His most recent books are *Priesthood Power—Blessing the Sick and the Afflicted; Rescuing Wayward Children;* and *The Shepherd Song.*

He and his wife, Elizabeth, have ten children and a growing number of grandchildren. They live in Orem, Utah. Read more of his writings at Meridian Magazine.com.

www.ingramcontent.com/pod-product-compliance
Lightning Source LLC
Chambersburg PA
CBHW080443110426
42743CB00016B/3256